BECOMING BEAUTIFUL

Becoming Beautiful

Ballroom Dance in the American Heartland

JOANNA BOSSE

UNIVERSITY OF ILLINOIS PRESS
Urbana, Chicago, and Springfield

Manufactured in the United States of America
1 2 3 4 5 C P 5 4 3 2 1
∞ This book is printed on acid-free paper.

Companion video material for this book is available at http://www.press.uillinois.edu/books/bosse/becoming_beautiful/.

Library of Congress Cataloging-in-Publication Data
Bosse, Joanna.
Becoming beautiful : ballroom dance in the American heartland / Joanna Bosse.
pages cm
Includes bibliographical references and index.
ISBN 978-0-252-03901-0 (hardcover : alk. paper) —
ISBN 978-0-252-08063-0 (pbk. : alk. paper) —
ISBN 978-0-252-09698-3 (e-book)
1. Ballroom dancing—Middle West—History. I. Title.
GV1751.B67 2015
793.3'3—dc23 2014025923

for christopher and ellery

CONTENTS

ACKNOWLEDGMENTS

When I began my doctoral work, I naïvely overlooked the fact that I would likely be required to write a book someday. Had I remembered, I certainly would have dropped out immediately, for writing a book is simply too daunting a task for one to undertake alone. Fortunately, I did not have to do it alone, but with the support of a great many people who advised, inspired, encouraged, cajoled, intimidated, distracted, understood, and loved.

To the Regent Dancers . . . your names were often the last thing I learned about you—after I learned your balance, your frame, your scent, the way you breathe, whether you start from a dead stop or move from audience to dancer in one fluid flow of steps. I knew your favorite partners, your favorite dances, your favorite steps long before I learned the names of your children or what you did for a living. Thanks to all of you for dancing with me and for sharing your stories. In particular, Bruce Leasure, David Owen, Eduardo Mendoza, John Hayes, Liz and Phil Meadows, Mark Balzer, Sheena Beaverson, Jeff Grossman, and Tom Case invested considerable time with me over many years, serving as central teachers and guides and sounding boards at every step. To David and Ellen Lin, it was only after I left central Illinois and no longer had a dancing home that I truly understood the gift that you have given to me. Thank you for sharing with me your wisdom, your generosity, your friendship, and for welcoming me into your family.

To my academic advisors, mentors, and teachers I owe an immeasurable debt of gratitude for guiding my intellectual development and for sharing so generously with their time and support. Bruno Nettl graciously answered the letter of a young and naïve student already two years into a doctorate in a different field, and soon thereafter I was his advisee and on the path to becoming an ethnomusicologist. Even on the most burdensome days, I love this field and will be forever grateful to him for ushering me into it. As one reads through this manuscript, it will be obvious the degree to which I am intellectually indebted to Thomas Turino. Tom was the first scholar to ever call me "a dancer," and he was unwavering in his support. My intellectual sensibility bears the stamp of his influence, and if this book contains anything that is useful, it is evidence of his mentorship. Versions of this work have been shared with teachers, colleagues, friends, and students and have benefited from their feedback and encouragement, including: Marsha Brofka-Barends, Elizabeth Branch-Dyson, Donna Buchanan, Cynthia Oliver, Anna Schultz, Heather White, and Genevieve Creedon. Thanks also to the undergraduate research assistants who provided academic and administrative support for this project, including Elizabeth Abeles-Allison, Elena Dunckel, Abriel Ferreira, Rebecca Helgeson, Julia Kramer, Linnea Jimisen, and Ben Thorp. The anonymous readers contracted by the press provided insightful, critically constructive, and detailed feedback. I am grateful for their ability to read the manuscript with a generosity of spirit that helped me carry the project to completion.

I have had the good fortune to teach at a number of supportive institutions, and at each I found colleagues, administrators, staff, and students to sustain me as I attempted to write a book while living in what seemed like an endless state of transition. I would like to thank the faculty, staff, students, and administrators in the School of Music at Millikin University, the Department of Music at Bowdoin College, the Music Department at the College of William and Mary, and the Residential College of the Arts and Humanities and College of Music at Michigan State University. In particular, I am thankful to these friend-colleagues, without whose wisdom, good humor, coffee breaks, and hijinks I would certainly have finished this book in half the time: Ray Boehmer, Mary Ellen Poole, JR Fralick, Birgit Tautz, Carmen Greenlee, Mary Hunter, Jim McCalla, Linda Marquis, Ann Folino-White, Kate McGormley, and Scot Yoder. I offer a special thanks to Michael Largey and Stephen Esquith for being the most honest, supportive, and generous mentors and colleagues I could imagine. The work was supported by a Fletcher Family Research Award from Bowdoin College and a Faculty Research Leave from the Residential College of the Arts and Humanities at Michigan State University. Material in chapter 5 appeared previously in the *Journal of American Folklore* and is reprinted with permission ("Whiteness and the Performance of Race in American Ballroom Dance," *Journal of American Folklore* 120 [475]: 19–47).

Most important, I want to thank my family. To my parents, Harold and Sharon Bosse: As a child I rolled my eyes from embarrassment and boredom as Dad launched once again into his litany of career advice that always ended with the mantra, "It is important to do what you enjoy." Despite appearances, I was paying attention, and even in the most frustrating moments it feels downright luxurious to be spending my days reading, writing, and teaching (though perhaps not grading). Thank you for working so hard, Mom and Dad, at jobs I suspect you did not enjoy all that much, while taking care of five children so that I may live this life. And thanks to my siblings Rena, John, Brenda, and Sharon Irene who remind me that the academy should only be a small part of it.

I am not sure if there is a word for the kind of writer I am: one who needs to sound out every concept and its application with an audience to work it through; but my method had serious implications for my husband and colleague, Christopher Scales. In addition to having read multiple drafts of this manuscript, he heard hundreds more while eating breakfast or driving to work or cleaning the kitchen. I am not entirely sure he understood what he was in for when he signed on with me, but I could not be more grateful that he did. The valuable lessons I have learned from his constancy, intellect, patience and love have proved more valuable than any the academy could provide.

To my daughter, Ellery: I have been distracted by this book since the day you entered my life, and I am sorry you have competed with it for my time and my attention. "Mom, put down the computer," you begged, commanded, chastened. I will make it up to you now, and I promise from here on out to be useless and unproductive in every way save being your loving Mother.

BECOMING BEAUTIFUL

I am not suggesting that dance experiences in themselves can change someone's political attitudes, because it is what people make of their experience that counts; but I argue that in particular contexts some forms of dancing are more likely than others to stimulate people's imagination and expand their consciousness, because of what they involve in terms of body movement, social interaction, and a challenge to previous experience. Just as some dance teachers insist that one moves as one thinks, so a change of movement may generate a change of mind.

—JOHN BLACKING, "MOVEMENT, DANCE, AND MUSIC AND THE VENDA GIRLS' INITIATION CYCLE"

Introduction

BECOMING BEAUTIFUL

In 2006 executives of the successful reality television show *Dancing with the Stars* caused a stir when they announced that Jerry Springer would perform in season 3. The oft-maligned host of a daytime television talk show renowned for its brawls and broken hearts cut an unsympathetic figure for fans of the show. As entertainment reporter Maria Caccia (2006) wrote in an article during that season, "I had never watched *Dancing with the Stars* until my sisters got me hooked, but when I heard that one of this season's contestants was to be Jerry Springer, I became nauseous. I mean, did I want to see this guy dance? The Sultan of Salaciousness? The King of Trash TV? Could I put up with that just to see Mario Lopez's dimples and Emmitt Smith's gorgeous smile?" To hear Springer's own telling, this reaction was not unlike the response of his partner, professional dancer Kym Johnson, upon hearing that she was paired with Springer for season 3.

But the sixty-four-year-old Springer held on week after week, claiming that even though the workouts were brutal, he was dedicated to learning how to waltz in order to dance with his special-needs daughter, Katie, at her upcoming wedding. His willingness to commit to the performance, even if in occasional self-deprecation or parody, slowly converted audiences, and they repeatedly voted for him to remain on the show even as better dancers were voted off. As Caccia states, "I admit I had Jerry all wrong, and like a lot of other Americans who watch *Dancing with the Stars*, I've fallen hard for Jerry Springer: father, dancer, trash-talk show host, and a man whose name is the title of an opera where people sing expletives on high notes." The audience's change of heart was sealed in week 4, when Springer performed one of the most memorable scenes in the history of the program. After dancing a competent waltz with Johnson to Patti Page's "Can I Have this Dance?" Springer caused members of both the cast and the audience to tear up as he walked into the audience to hug his daughter, Katie, before returning to his partner's side for judging.[1]

Springer lasted three more weeks beyond this performance, finally being eliminated in week seven. When it was announced that he was going home, the crowd began chanting Springer's name in the manner of his daytime talk show audiences.

HOST TOM BERGERON: "They're cheering your name, but I would expect that they're cheering a different Jerry Springer than they thought they knew seven weeks ago."

COHOST BROOKE BURKE: "Jerry, I can tell right now that you're getting a little verklempt. You're touched by this. But you've been a mayor, you're a successful talk-show host. How has being a ballroom dancer compared?"

AUDIENCE MEMBER: [interrupts] "We love you Jerry!"

SPRINGER: "And I love you. [audience laughs] I, uh, it's . . . [becomes misty and then pauses to regain composure]. This is unbelievable. I hope everyone has a moment in life where . . ." [breaks into tears].

[The entire audience sighs in sympathy, as does his partner, Kym Johnson, who also gives him a hug and then steps in to finish the interview.]

JOHNSON: "I've had so much fun. It's been absolutely amazing meeting Jerry. He's just the nicest man I've ever met. And he's really put himself into this competition and he started off not being able to dance at all, and he's been able to do every dance. I've had a ball, and I've been able to meet such a beautiful person."

Even after taking into consideration the emotionally manipulative and scripted nature of reality television, Springer's appearances on the show inspired an overwhelming sentimentality. Jerry Springer, one of the most unsavory characters to perform in the history of the show, was made into a "beautiful person," one America "fell hard" for, through ballroom performance. This is the story that Springer's partner, Kym Johnson, authored to make sense of her experience coming to know him through dance, and it was corroborated by audiences who witnessed this experience on television.

Jerry Springer's journey from beginner to competent dancer and his metamorphosis into "a different Jerry Springer" testify to a belief in and commitment to "becoming beautiful" and the power of transformation that my informants also believed to be inherent in performing ballroom dance.[2] Springer's story exemplifies one I heard repeatedly among the midwestern ballroom dancers I worked with: that dancing makes them feel beautiful. Based on ethnographic fieldwork with a local community of amateur ballroom dancers in rural Illinois, this book endeavors to understand the narrative of becoming beautiful and its relationship to the experience that inspires it.

The dancers discussed herein decided in their adulthood to become dancers, long after many habits of self-identification assumed a position of tacit authority, and long after they came to believe that they, in fact, did not dance. For a small number of individuals, the decision to dance posed no significant challenge to their sense of self; perhaps they took ballet as a child or came of age during the swing era. But for most, the decision to dance publicly, to become a dancer, was one wrought with varying degrees of nervous anxiety and fear of embarrassment, failure, exposure, or rejection. Whether excited at the possibility or afraid of the consequences, whether comforted by the companionship of a spouse or feeling conspicuously alone, individuals entered the dance hall and set foot to music. Aspirations of becoming—becoming graceful, physically and sexually proficient, and healthy individuals with deep and satisfying connections to others—fueled the desire to dance. Something about the experience of moving in a musical world affirmed my informants' hopes that this kind of experience was possible through dance.

In the epigraph that opens this introduction, John Blacking, a pioneer in the ethnomusicological study of movement, weaves together experience, identity, and the power of dance to transform identity practices. He suggests that dance is capable of stimulating people's imagination and expanding their awareness, especially when it provides a challenge to previous experience. Dance thus creates the potential for a transformation that integrates individual moving bodies and large-scale social movements, the corporeal and the conceptual, and individual subjectivity and community ethos. This ethnographic account of a specific community of midwestern ballroom dancers is a story of such a transformation, a change of mind and of self, following a change in movement. Unlike the many excellent ethnomusicological works on traditions deeply seeded in cultural heritage and ancestry, this story is one of finding new traditions and creating new identities—certainly embedded in established cultural norms, but setting new paths nevertheless. Thus this ethnography documents both what is and what one hopes to become.

This book emerged from a set of basic questions about amateur ballroom dance. Following the lead of Manuel Peña (1985), who suggests that a change in artistic practice can be understood as a class of solutions to a social problem, I wondered: what social work did these individuals accomplish by choosing to dance? Given that few of my informants grew up dancing or ever feeling themselves capable of dance, why did they choose to dance at all? And why, of all things, did they choose ballroom? The genre is rich with rules and codes, categories and classifications, a complicated lexicon and pedagogy, and is, as one informant joked, "codified down to a gnat's ass." How did this extensive rationalization of performance connect to the immediate and visceral experience of actually dancing?

Becoming Beautiful investigates the genre and the transformative experiences it provides for amateur dancers. Approaching the "transformation trope" of becoming beautiful as an articulation, or what Victor Turner and Edward Bruner (1986) termed an "expression" of an experience that otherwise escapes language, I argue that the contemporary performance of ballroom dance among amateurs generates feelings of positive personal transformation, of becoming beautiful, because it dissolves the actual and the ideal, the shared and the individual, into a singular rich and moving experience. I also demonstrate how certain generic conventions, themselves "expressions" of a sort, might facilitate such responses. In doing so, the book is an exploration into the relationship between dancing as a material, embodied, visceral, cerebral, and emotional experience and the stories that emerge to make sense of that experience.

"Becoming beautiful" is a densely compacted verbal expression that gives voice to the concern my informants had for the relationship between social values and embodied social identities. It functioned as a leitmotif of sorts, employed by dancers to articulate how aspects of identity were physically encoded and expressed both through movement on the dance floor and in the ways they talked about dance. Individuals performed notions of their own gender, race, and class, dancing contingent social identities over and again, shaping and refiguring their bodies and, in so doing, ideas about what their bodies mean and who they are. They also reflected on the experience of doing so, using varying kinds of language to communicate about that experience not only through their reflections with me and fellow dancers, but also with the terminology, labels, and pedagogies they employ. My goal is to suss out how these social-identity categories are embodied, performed, and conceived in particular ways, some highlighted and others downplayed under the guise of beauty.

Recent ethnomusicological work on dance and movement has brought the nature of artistic performance as an embodied experience into the center of focus and in so doing has illuminated a different path for ethnomusicological pursuits: to consider the physical experience of responding to music and the materiality of performance (Friedson 1996; Hagedorn 2001; Hahn 2007; Kisliuk 1998). While not the only ethnomusicologists interested in embodiment, dance scholars have certainly been on the vanguard of embodiment work within musicological scholarship, ushering in innovative and experimental techniques for ethnographic research and writing, shifting the focus from musicians to the individuals responding to music in social context, and inviting us all to consider performance as a physical act with material consequences: sweat, muscle, fatigue, heightened states of awareness, and the like. Dance studies reveal to us how music is experienced in/by/with the body; how music is related to other cultural phenomena; and how it is understood by people who are non-music specialists. My own work emerges from this literature, inspired by the effort to better understand the experience of moving one's body through space to create something aesthetically as well as physically pleasing, and seeking to understand the different ways of being and knowing that dancers (and non-music specialists) bring to performance.

Becoming Beautiful and the Ethnomusicology of Experience

Academic engagement with the concept of beauty has a long history, and my goal here is not so much to connect with that body of literature as to speak to the use of the term as an emic framework dancers used to communicate what was meaningful about their dance experiences. I am not positing a particular definition of the term or characteristics that together constitute beauty in any kind of universal sense. Rather, I consider the ethnographic trope of becoming beautiful as an "expression" in the sense suggested by Victor Turner and Edward Bruner (1986) in their anthropological work on experience.

Turner and Bruner distinguish two elements of experience: the everyday reality of lived experience (Dilthy's *erlebnis*) and an experience, an articulation about an experience framed in the telling, which they call "expression." In short, "expression" in this sense is the story we tell about our experience, whether those stories are with words, song, visual images, or gesture. The two, experience and expression, are bound together, and the relationship between them is dialectical and dialogic (6).

Turner and Bruner make the case for experience by noting that experience is different from behavior, which implies an outside observer and standardized routines. Experience is more intimate, more active, and more self-referential and includes actions, feelings, gesture, and the products of them as well as the reflections about them. We describe an other's behavior, we have an experience.[3] This distinction resonates with the history of dance scholarship in ethnomusicology, which has seen a move from the description of dance as visual spectacle to intimate portraits of the dance subject—from third person to first person.[4]

A focus on experience also shifts the focus from the corporate, or collective and shared aspects of culture and performance, to the individual experience of them. This is difficult work to do, because experience, by its very nature, is specific to each individual and involves not only the "what happens" but how individuals understand it. The participant-observer model of ethnography is ideally suited to the task, synthesizing the collection of data about the experiences of the people we study (documenting their experiences and gathering their stories in various articulations) with knowledge gained of the experience through participation in the event itself. Integrating analysis about with knowledge of in meaningful and illuminating ways has been a cornerstone of ethnomusicological inquiry since its early conversations about bi-musicality (Hood 1960). In more recent years, scholars have collated their own experiences into the ethnomusicological narrative in order to take us beyond the notion of fluency in vernacular systems gained through experience and into an understanding of the embodied and subjective nature of that cultural knowledge and of experience itself (see, for example, Barz and Cooley 2008; Hagadorn 2001; Hahn 2007; Kisliuk 1998).

Taking Turner and Bruner's two-part model of experience as my starting point, I aim to understand how one expression, the narrative of becoming beautiful, is connected to the experience it represents—the moments where experience and expression connect and where the dialogue is sparked. For instance, how or why might the physical sensation of feeling the momentum of one's own body moving through space to music become described as having "become beautiful?"

The book takes its name from this faith in the transformative properties of ballroom dance as articulated in the particular expression, "becoming beautiful." Not only did dancers feel the genre itself was beautiful, but they felt that performing it made them beautiful as well. Beauty was the centerpiece of performance for the dancers I worked with, the goal to which they aspired, and the concept was employed in multiple ways. The first is perhaps one of the most obvious meanings: a reference to physical beauty and its attainment. Over and again, dancers testified to ballroom's miraculous power to make them feel, literally, more beautiful. To paraphrase one dancer, "I enter the dance as a klutz, and by the end I'm beautiful." The emotional impact of such a transformation can be overwhelming, and in fact many of my interviews ended in tears, as individuals gave voice to the deep feelings of insecurity that are soothed by the healing properties of dance. In a society that values the outward, visible signs of physical perfection regardless of the cost to health and emotional well-being, the individuals I worked with—average, middle-class Americans—grappled with their own physical imperfections on a daily basis. Ballroom dance provided a respite from those feelings of inadequacy and unattractiveness that trouble the daily lives of many average Americans.

Becoming beautiful extended beyond feeling beautiful (in the subjective sense), however, to feeling more desired by another person, especially to members of the opposite sex. Single men, in particular, testified that they took up ballroom dance as a way to meet women and learn how to interact with them. Ethan's[5] testimony was not uncommon: "I started dancing because I wanted to learn how to touch women." This is true even for those who entered the ballroom with a spouse. I heard the phrase "ballroom dance saved my marriage" so often that I considered using it for the title of this book. Middle-aged couples overwhelmed with children and careers, having lost sight of their own sexuality and that of their spouse as well, sought common ground in the ballroom. They sought feelings of connectedness, desirability, and affection, and found it through ballroom dance. As Mark states:

> Ballroom dance probably saved my marriage, . . . what was happening was, we didn't have a home base to connect to, where there was something that didn't have to do with the kids or my work or the house, . . . we needed something that we could do together and could just enjoy. And so, we both came out here, and the way David taught the class, "Have fun, don't be critical, don't worry if it doesn't happen right away" . . . there wasn't any pressure. There wasn't any pressure to do it right. There wasn't any right or wrong yet for us because we weren't anywhere near where we could begin to know what was right. And the very clearly defined roles for social dancing—the men are leading and the women are following, and the act of leading was the art of giving invitations and then following what she does with those invitations. It was kind of, "Wow, this is something that you have to work together at. You have to be on the same page."

Likewise, Jane was surprised by the effect dancing had on her relationship with her husband, with whom collaboration was usually a tense affair:

> To tell you the truth, in other areas of our life there was a lot of tension. At that time, you know, marriages sort of follow these paths, and we were at a time when there was some real tension. Dancing eased that. We were able to really enjoy ourselves, enjoy one another. There was something that . . . I don't know, we had the same reaction that when we started dancing we would just break out into a big grin. You know, it was just so happy.

And so ballroom dance involved more than a transformation of self: it involved the transformation of relationships as well, with increased feelings of connection with a romantic partner.

With the theme of beauty my informants also addressed the importance of aesthetic values and the process by which they are conceived and articulated. The genre is collective, and no small amount of satisfaction is derived from the act of participation. However, concern for an audience and the visual aspects of performance drive the genre's governing aesthetic principles. Ballroom dance involves an explicit set of stylistic criteria set in place to promote a visually arresting performance influenced by the classical arts of Western Europe. And so the idea of becoming beautiful also spoke to the act of using one's body as a medium for artistic expression to the end of realizing an aesthetically pleasing visual spectacle.

Finally, with their emphasis on becoming beautiful, rather than *being* beautiful, dancers highlighted the contingent nature of identity and a sense that their "true" selves were emergent and conjured through the act of dancing. The temporal and temporary nature of performance resonated with the ways that dancers moved between various and varying notions of self conception, or what I term below the "self-imaginary."[6]

In sum, beauty served as a marker for that which was believed to be most valuable and desirable in the social world of the dancers with whom I worked. Becoming beautiful served as a gloss for the development of a more embodied experience, including alternative models for sexual, gendered, and racialized identities that are generated and, paradoxically, transcended in the thrill of the dance moment. This more-embodied self enjoyed greater self-acceptance and sometimes the perception of being more accepted by fellow community members. Beauty was an idea dense with meaning, and their choice of it as the stance they used to consider their performance encapsulates these many different senses of the term (Berger 2009).

The feeling of dancing is an embodied, experiential performance of values, of what dancers believe goodness is, and of, as I will suggest in the last chapter, a state of awareness in which their intention and their actions are one, moving fluidly through the world in intimate conversation with another without society's critiques sounding in their own internal voice. Moving in this way feels good—that is, it feels both pleasurable and right. "Becoming beautiful" is one common way that dancers described this experience, and I employ it here as a guide to an understanding of this experience. The rest of this book provides details of what it meant to become beautiful, with each chapter documenting how, through dance, individuals became more aware of and connected to their corporeality, and how they used the language of ballroom dance as a social frame for making sense of the changes wrought about by their experience. Dancers derived a great deal of joy and satisfaction from this endeavor, and this important fact wends its way through this work.

The Self-Imaginary

The "self-imaginary" is a concept I have developed to aid in my understanding of the ways in which social beings understand themselves and their potential as distinct from "identity," which is collectively negotiated and socially valent. Identity, as defined by practice theorists such as Bourdieu (1977) and Giddens (1979) as habits for action and thought, is therefore fed by the self-imaginary, the well of intellectual and creative resources that individuals choose from when determining their thoughts, actions, and habits. The self-imaginary is the way we understand our own identity and potential—who we are but also who we possess the potential to become, provided certain conditions. Some of these ideas may not be observable or manifest in practice. I employ the term to name the ways in which individuals understand and identify their sense of selfhood, potential, and trajectory of personal development. Unlike identities that are collectively negotiated and agreed upon, the self-imaginary is the purview of the individual and subject alone. It is the cognitive, emotional, and embodied space where one harbors senses of the self that others may not agree with and ideas about one's past and future potential. As such, it may provide more contextual information for why an individual acts in a certain way than the more observable aspects of identity ever can.

Although the notion of identity has been a powerful one in ethnography, it suggests a kind of stasis that runs counter to the sense of emergent identity from which my informants generally operated. I am not speaking about the processual nature of identity construction that has been noted in scholarly work since the 1980s so much as I am about the ethnographically grounded conception of self as it is conceived by middle-class Americans. In this lay sense, the self is understood in several different and discrete ways. All are conceptual in nature and depend on culling characteristics and habits of thought, body, and behavior. The first is the self as it is understood to exist at any given moment. The second is the ideal self the individual imagines and desires herself to be capable of developing into. The third is an emergent middle ground of transition—of becoming the ideal—between the first two categories. They are all a part of the self-imaginary—the range of qualities, behaviors, thoughts, and desires.

The booming self-help and personal-growth industries in the United States—evident in talk shows, magazines, and other popular culture media—capitalize on this sense of duality between a current flawed self and an ideal self, attainable through attention and work. As I put the final touches on this chapter, Oprah Winfrey's final campaign, "Live Your Best Life," is being promoted in all programs offered on her television show, television network, Web site, satellite radio station, and in her magazine, *O*. The notion is that individuals are capable of living a better (indeed, best) life should they awaken to and develop their potential. The issue is not so much one of change but of excavation. Women, in particular, are asked not to change and become "someone else" but to tap the potential they already possess to become their "true selves" (Winfrey's language).

The imagination plays an important role in this conception of self and the process of tapping potential. In various iterations, individuals are instructed to use their imagination to mentally picture their new and improved selves as they walk through their world, encounter and relate to other people, and take on new challenges in their personal and professional lives. In the personal testimonies you will read throughout this book, you will learn that for many of my informants, both women and men, the process of learning how to dance required a faith in the potential most had not yet realized, and some thought nonexistent. Following on this initial impulse, they eventually signed up for dance classes and made good on this sense of untapped potential.

In academic terms, I might suggest, as Judith Butler has, that any sense of the self is a construction, a "sense" that is rooted in the imagined existence of a preexisting interiority that does not necessarily exist. So, the dual sense of self that I have suggested here—essentially The Who One Believes Herself to Be and The Who One Believes Herself to Be Capable of Becoming—is also a fabrication. Perhaps this is so, but it has proved to be a powerful way to conceive of the human experience for the individuals I have worked with, and if its ubiquitous presence in American popular culture suggests anything, it seems to be a powerful cognitive framework for millions of middle-class Americans living today. Informed and motivated by the self-imaginary—beliefs about who we are, who we have been, and who we could be—our actions represent a process of becoming, though perhaps never being.

Affinity Groups

This study diverges from more conventional ethnomusicological counterparts in that it does not focus on a particular bounded community or subgroup that recognizes a similar cultural, racial, national, or ethnic heritage; nor does it frame its topic as an expression of such cultural affinity, even if translocal in nature. Rather than a form of cultural knowledge that is passed from one generation to its youth, American ballroom is, for the most part, a practice that some adults elect to do in their adulthood, not because it expresses their cultural heritage or who they think they are, but precisely because it is a departure from their everyday lives up to that point.[7] Borrowing the term "affinity group" from the political sphere, I use it to discuss the particular qualities of a selective social configuration embedded within larger cultural and subcultural formations. Affinity groups such as the Regent "family"—a social group formed exclusively through performance—do not necessarily comprise people who live in the same community. Likewise, they do not necessarily self-identify along the same race or ethnic lines, nor are they necessarily citizens of the same country. Because of this, ballroom itself is not reduced to an expression of any of these kinds of identity categories, although these identities inform ballroom performance in multiple ways.

In this way "ballroomers" are different from members of other North American dance communities I have encountered. Many of the Latino and Latina salsa dancers I met said that dancing salsa was a way to connect to their cultural heritage; likewise, I spoke with country two-step dancers who loved country music and dance because it expressed their rural, agricultural lifestyles or self-proclaimed working-class "white trash" sensibilities. This is not to say that ballroom, as a genre rooted in the popular traditions of Western Europe and Euro-America, did not arise from a particular cultural context and shared cultural predispositions, but rather that it was not the subject of such explicit strategic essentialism at my fieldsite. Furthermore, given its long history, its spread throughout the world, and the diversity of its participants, ballroom dance today defies one-to-one correlation with any specific cultural group and resists affiliation with any one region.[8] In fact, the cultural diversity of ballroom dancers across contexts was used by dancers to make claims for the genre's universality.

Affinity groups, especially those composed of amateur performers, are a common element of dance and music contexts and yet remain undertheorized within ethnomusicological and ethnochoreological works. This study contributes to the literature on such groups and provides detailed ethnographic data on their formation. What is notable about affinity groups, at least those treated in the scant ethnomusicological literature on the topic, is that social class often functions as the predominant vector of shared identity, albeit a tacit one, for the group.[9] This is certainly true for the ballroom dancers with whom I have worked, a fact that will receive greater attention in chapter 1. What is also notable about the Regent "family" and affinity groups in general is that they are cultural formations seeking to forge a new identity that is not expressly cultural in nature. Furthermore, they do so through performance.

Research and Method

This ethnography centers on a group of amateur ballroom dancers from the Regent Ballroom in Savoy, Illinois. Savoy is a small, affluent community in central Illinois, just a few miles south of Champaign-Urbana and the main campus of the University of Illinois. During my fieldwork, Savoy was home to forty-five hundred residents, with a median household income of $48,500 and a median home value of $147,100. The community was more than 80 percent white, 6 percent East Asian, and 5 percent black. With an unemployment rate of 1.2 percent, 59 percent of Savoy's residents were college graduates, while 31 percent possessed professional or graduate degrees (the U.S. average at the time of my fieldwork was 8.9 percent).[10] Most of Savoy's residents worked for the University of Illinois or private companies in nearby Champaign, or were self-employed. Although Savoy lies in close proximity to the slightly more economically and racially diverse towns of Champaign and Urbana, the ballroom dancers at the Regent generally reflected the demographics of Savoy in terms of race and socioeconomic status. They were predominantly white, with a small number of dancers of Asian, African American, and Latin American descent.

The Regent is a commercial space that offered (for an admission fee) two dances per week, eight to ten dance classes per week, as well as private lessons, and the sale of pedagogical videos and dance shoes. It is also a banquet space leased for wedding receptions, corporate functions, exercise classes, and the like. It is owned and operated by David Lin, who handles all aspects of the dance business. A former ballroom dance competitor, he created the curriculum, deejays the dances, and teaches most of the classes. David is a middle-aged Chinese immigrant who arrived in North America as a teenager. He moved to Illinois from his family's home in Toronto, Canada, to attend the University of Illinois. He settled in the area permanently to teach dance, eventually married his wife, Ellen (a white woman hailing from a small farm community in southern Illinois), and has recently become an American citizen. Ellen is co-owner of the Regent, manages the banquet center, and keeps the books.

On the suggestion of a fellow graduate student who knew of my research interests, I went to the Regent Ballroom for the first time in January 1996 to consider it as a possible fieldsite for a graduate seminar research paper.[11] While I was an experienced country two-step dancer, I had never before performed ballroom dance. However, after several graduate seminar research papers on the topic, it was clear that the Regent was a fruitful research site for me, and deserving of a longer look.

Participant observation formed the basis of my research method. I conducted fieldwork in the dance clubs of central Illinois from 1996 to 2002, with follow-up trips in 2005 and 2011. I typically spent four nights per week at some type of dance event (a dance at a bar, club, ballroom, restaurant, or house party; a dance class; or a private lesson), and I spent additional time simply socializing with dancers or in some type of formal or informal interview. Prior to heading out for a night of social dancing, I attended one or more dance classes a week, which were offered in the early evening, and spent afternoons in private lessons or interviews. I learned to perform every genre taught at the Regent by completing almost all of the dance courses offered there and through private lessons with David. Social dancing allows for a great deal of conversation as well as dancing, and I learned much from dancers during these impromptu discussions, often sparked by reactions to a given musical selection or the dance moves of a passing couple. I also conducted formal interviews, which I documented with audio or video recordings, and engaged a number of dancers in ongoing e-mail discussions. In 2002 I received ninety responses to a voluntary survey of Regent dancers.

The unbounded nature of fieldwork in a commercial venue makes the quantification of research participants somewhat difficult. The Regent's client roster included more than one thousand households. Offering at least two courses per evening, five nights per week, as well as two social dance events, the Regent caters to patrons who come and go with regularity. Attendance at the popular Friday evening dances, of which I attended more than two hundred, varied depending on the time of year and generally ranged from 150 to 250 dancers. Over the seven years of my fieldwork research, I spoke and danced with literally hundreds of dancers, and most "regulars" to the Regent events knew me on a first-name basis.

In addition to dancing and learning, I also worked at the Regent in a variety of other capacities—as a bartender, receptionist for dance events, support staff for wedding parties, labor for small renovation projects, and eventually as private teacher and occasional deejay or teaching assistant. When David first decided to host salsa dance events, I worked the door, managed the basic operations of the club, and closed up at the end of the night. These experiences were useful to my research, but they also provided a necessary financial boost. David and I bartered for services. I worked for him in these contexts and in turn was afforded entrance into dances and classes; I also earned money to purchase shoes and other dance equipment.[12]

This study is based on my ethnographic fieldwork experiences living and dancing with "ballroomers" in central Illinois, and their real-life stories drive the one I tell with this book. Where possible, *Becoming Beautiful* extends its purview beyond this contemporary account of a specific and localized dance community to consider a larger, national context throughout the American twentieth century, but it is, first and foremost, an ethnography of the transformative power of dance and music.

The following chapters appear in an order that models, albeit roughly, my own induction into ballroom dance. The genre has been subjected to good-natured ribbing about its strict adherence to rules and classification systems in feature films such as *Strictly Ballroom*, *Shall We Dance?*, and *Dirty Dancing*. Chapter 1 examines these various classificatory systems, providing an overview of their content and suggesting that they articulate dancers' class disposition and, particularly, the betwixt-and-between-ness that characterizes the American middle class.

Chapter 2 takes us into the dance hall as a social space where disparate groups come together to move in synchrony. As a zone for aesthetic expression as well as commerce, the dance hall structures experience and feelings of comfort, safety, and creativity: to become beautiful requires a safe space wherein dancers can make themselves vulnerable to one another. This chapter locates my case study within a small-town entertainment industry, challenging prevailing notions about the commerce of performance that are based largely on urban and transnational contexts. Chapter 3 outlines the nature of partnership and connection and the craft of leading and following. In addition to describing how men and women related to one another on and off the floor, it discusses the rhetorical and performative strategies dancers used to reconfigure ballroom's conventional role in constructing gender and heterosexual normativity in movement and sound—actively engaging problematic and antiquated aspects of beauty and resignifying them with contemporary sensibilities about equity and connection.

Chapter 4 provides an analysis of the cornerstone genres, the Standard and Latin dances, in order to reveal the ways in which race intersects with class in this context. It discusses more tacit aspects of ballroom dance, race, whiteness, and exoticism, and how these embodied (and seemingly "natural") aspects of identity are encoded as different aspects of beauty through ballroom dance. It suggests that white universality is expressed through the large genre subdivisions of Standard, Latin, and Nightclub, and focuses on how these categories and the discourse that surrounds them articulate notions of race, self, and other.

The concluding chapter threads the major themes of the text back to notions of beauty and experience—the act of becoming beautiful through performance. It locates ballroom's transformative potential in the affective experience of synchronized performance particular to this form of couple dancing, which stimulates the imagination of one's ideal self, reifies a belief in the success of the pursuit, and serves to naturalize the social constructions of class, gender, and race on which such notions are based.

Interspersed throughout the text are descriptive interludes from my own dance experiences at the Regent Ballroom, and together they depict the events of a typical Friday night dance—an important weekly ritual at my fieldsite. The events described in these stories did occur, though not necessarily on the same night. They are representative of my experiences having attended close to two hundred such dances.

Including these stories in this manner provides an opportunity for ethnographic description beyond the more explicitly argument-based narrative that occurs within the chapters. Given the very individual and isolated quality of ballroom dance—for no one on the outside can fully know what occurs between any given dancing couple (and indeed even the two partners in a couple may have differing interpretations of what happens)—I detail some aspects of my own dance experiences here to communicate something of what it is like to partner with another ballroom dancer (Sklar 1991, 2000). As such, this personalized "thick description" also communicates the nature of my subject position and my relationship to the dancers with whom I worked (Geertz 1973). And finally, it affords an opportunity to provide ethnographic detail that may not be accounted for in the more explicitly analytical chapters. This approach eschews the traditional use of ethnographic data to craft and support an argument and suggests that this case study, as any, cannot be a complete accounting. Furthermore, a short documentary film and video examples of the various dance genres discussed herein can be found at http://www.press.uillinois.edu/books/bosse/becoming_beautiful/. This material, most of it shot at the Regent Ballroom and surrounding area, is offered to bring readers even more deeply into the story and to aid in using the book for teaching purposes.

Finally, I aim to provoke my readers, both the professional academics as well as the ballroom dancers. Ballroom dance is most often associated with American middle- and upper-middle-class whites—a group that has evaded extensive ethnomusicological inquiry.[13] My decision to turn a fairly conventional ethnographic gaze on this group will likely discomfort ethnographers of music and dance as well as ballroom dancers. In doing so, I hope to call into question the problematic assumptions and racial underpinnings of the ethnographic project, challenge our intellectual habits for what an informant looks like, and deepen our collective sensitivity for how it feels to be one. By employing conventional narratives regarding the ethnographic subject, the ethnographer's relationship to his/her subject, what it is to be an informant, and the role of our work in the larger sociopolitical context in which it is conducted, I strive to disturb and recast those narratives with the hope of encouraging more dialogue about how to improve our methods, reveal our biases, and reflect on our conclusions and contributions to the larger academic community.

Interlude

By 8:00 the dancers have filled the lobby. They are lining up to pay the $6 cover charge to Genevieve, pick up their dance card, and head for the floor. The dance card serves as a program, listing the order of the genres in groups of two, each grouping called a set, as well as announcements about upcoming events. As dancers hang their coats and change into their dance shoes—soft, supple leather with suede bottoms—they greet each other warmly and tell stories of their week. Sylvia, a real estate agent with two adult children, arrives with her new husband Jimmy—a name I have given him because, if possible, Jimmy Stewart would have played him in the film version of their story. Jimmy is a sweet, smart, handsome, and uncomplicated man. He is a successful professional, a good dancer, and it is absolutely clear that he loves Sylvia. He is a classic example of what might be known colloquially as "a catch."

The two met here at the Regent and continue to dance weekly. We all began dancing around the same time, and we went through several dance classes together. I have danced often with Jimmy. He is a great dance partner in my estimation. No fancy moves, but always feels great—a confident lead, sensitive to my responses, and easy to be with. They both greet me warmly with a hug and a kiss on the cheek. Although we only know each other from the Regent, we speak as if we are old friends.

I sit down next to Sylvia in the lobby seating area, a newly remodeled space decorated in a muted citrus-yellow color scheme. It is so much more welcoming than the previous arrangement, walls clad in wood paneling and a large aquarium placed squarely in the middle of the entry, cutting off the coat closet. Rather than the dark, cave-like feeling, the space now is open and bright and inspires me to breathe a little more deeply, sit a little taller, and prepare to move with grand gestures.

Snuggling close to Sylvia, we are shoulder to shoulder changing into our dance shoes and looking over the photo album from their recent wedding—a late-summer affair in the backyard of their newly constructed suburban home. The two are nearing sixty years old, with adult children from previous marriages, and as I look over their photos, I recall an earlier conversation I had with Sylvia. She is a successful professional and expressed to me how worried she was to marry Jimmy. "I love him. This isn't the problem. But my divorce was tough, and I love the freedom I have now. I don't want to give it up." He sauntered into the conversation, addressing me, but clearly talking to her, "Look, I don't want her freedom. She can have it. She can come and go as she pleases, she can have her work and her fun. I just want her in my life, that's all." They knew my own love life was a mess at this point, and I nodded to say, "Yes, it's complicated." But Jimmy, a practical sort, shook his head in rebuttal. "It's not that tough. You find love. You choose love."

Eventually, Sylvia did choose to marry Jimmy, and now we look over their wedding photos. It is also my first opportunity to see pictures of their new home together—a large, brick colonial structure in a new Champaign suburb. Later in the season I will attend a holiday party at their home—soaring cathedral ceilings, gorgeously appointed with crystal and crown molding. The two will give me a tour, showing me their respective "hobby" rooms and guest spaces they hope will soon be visited by children and grandchildren. It is not the kind of home I am accustomed to myself—my own working-class background limited my access to these neighborhoods, and I have a hard time believing that people live day-to-day lives in such large and decorated houses.

After closing the photo album and receiving my congratulations, they once again inquire about my own love life. They are newlyweds, and like many newlyweds, believe deeply that everyone should know some measure of the love they feel for each other. Sylvia's eyes are warm and kind, and she looks deep into mine as if trying to address my heart directly. It feels so familial and intimate, and yet I really barely know them. I do not even know their last names. I have danced with them. This is the basis of our connection.

As the first strains of the waltz waft from the ballroom, we finish lacing our shoes and make our way past the front desk and the restrooms, down the corridor, around the large salt-water aquarium to the dance hall. The early minutes of the dance exude a quiet romance not only reserved for newlyweds. The Friday night ballroom dance is clearly date night for many couples in attendance. Arthur and Katherine, Dane and Luella, Tony and Sarah, all empty-nesters or retirees, looking to reconnect after investing decades in careers and child-rearing, or others like Sylvia and Jimmy who are working on their second or third marriage and determined not to make the same mistakes again. Their conversations are littered with loving glances, small gestures of affectionate intimacy, and the kind of good-natured ribbing only spouses can perpetrate. The affection is almost palpable—contagious. I feel as if somehow their affection for each other has rubbed off on me, and my own fondness for these people increases as I move among them.

Shivering in my sleeveless, lightweight blouse I make my way to David's deejay table. It is a cool, late-autumn evening, and the multiple sets of exterior doors found on three of the four walls of the ballroom are propped open to allow the cool breezes to chill the space. Eventually the room will be heated by the one hundred and fifty or so dancing bodies, and I will be thankful that David will turn on the ceiling fans, but now I am quite cold as I watch David settle in behind his deejay equipment.

"Hey, come check out my new setup!" he says. David is a technophile of all sorts: audio equipment, still and video cameras, computers, lighting. He loves it all. I jump up on the platform and look over his shoulder at the simple, seventeen-inch MacBook Pro that houses his deejay software and thousands of music tracks cataloged by dance genre. "Remember when I used to drag those cases with hundreds of CDs in them? Before you came around it used to be worse because I used LPs and turntables," he laughs. He hums to himself and snaps his fingers as he reviews the next few songs he will play. Even after years of working in this business, he seems roused by the Friday night dances, . . . like throwing his own party every week. After they are over he is awake for hours, unable to sleep from the energy of the nights' events.

This is an opportune spot for me because David talks to me as he plays songs, describing how he feels about a particular musical example or his students as they circle past him. He knows I am working on a research project on ballroom dancing, and enjoys talking to me, in a stream of consciousness, about his thoughts on dancing.

"Why don't you come over after the dance?" he asks me. "Tuan and I are cooking!" Tuan is a friend of David's, a godfather to his children, a violinist, and a social dancer married to one of the most accomplished competitors in the region. Tuan, an immigrant from Southeast Asia, and his Scandinavian wife, Sophia, live a few hours away but often return "home" to Champaign, where they completed their doctoral degrees in engineering, so that Sophia can practice with her competition partner, Steve. Tuan is one of the most creative, fun, and kind people I have ever met, and together, David and Tuan put on quite a feast of Asian cuisine. These "afterglow" parties are as much fun as the dancing, and some of the most enjoyable nights of my seven years in Champaign were spent sitting around David and Ellen's table watching David and Tuan cook for a small crowd of dance friends.

The tables near the deejay booth are largely the domain of singles, including the youngest constituency—university graduate students in their twenties and early thirties, most of whom are members of the university group, the Dancing Illini, as well as single and divorced professionals in their late forties and fifties. After chatting with David, I greet William, Dean, Leo, and the rest with a hug and kiss: not my way of greeting friends in other contexts, but appropriate here. In fact, one night some time before, while moving down the line, hugging and kissing as I went, I turned to see that the person I was reaching out for was not a Regent "regular" but a fellow musicologist from my graduate program who was there for the first time at the invitation of a friend. He looked in horror at the thought that he and I might not only touch, but actually embrace, and recoiled from my extended hand. This was a fellow classmate. I have been to his house a number of times, sat beside him in class, commiserated about our studies. But it was clear that touch was out of the question. The instance of rapid code-switching was instructive, and I imagined that for a number of my fellow dancers, the dance floor might be the only place where we greet our friends physically. Through dancing, we routinely inhabit each other's personal space. It is natural for me to hug and feel the warmth of their cheek on mine, and it feels right to me that I should physically "check-in" with them before we dance.

1

The Classification of Style

Pete, a retired, single dancer in his seventies and a regular attendee at the Regent's Friday night dances, leaned in close during our swing at a Friday night dance, and in a playful, conspiratorial tone said, "You know, I really think this is a foxtrot, but they get mad at me when I don't do what I'm supposed to," nodding to the deejay booth. Continuing the conspiratorial gag, I looked over my shoulder before leaning in to whisper, "I'm game. Let's do it." He smiled broadly, and we alternated between his own idiosyncratic versions of foxtrot and swing for the rest of the song.

Charmed by his sense of humor and his unwillingness to completely conform to social norms, I was always happy to dance with Pete. I danced most often with him at the Rose Bowl, a rough-and-tumble country music bar in Urbana, Illinois, where he was a fixture for the Sunday night performance of the house band, the Western Wheels. He felt more comfortable in the relaxed atmosphere of the Rose Bowl, and never once there did he signal me so explicitly that he was hoping to, or even about to, switch genres. At the Rose Bowl, he just did it. He was an unorthodox dancer, to be sure, mixing music and dance genres together in unconventional ways, switching between dance genres several times within one song, and performing steps of his own creation. For this reason, many women ballroom dancers felt great ambivalence about dancing with Pete. In fact, he had originally intended on asking Monica to dance this song with him, but when she saw him headed her way, she quickly ran for the restroom.

Pete's hesitance to dance a foxtrot to a musical example labeled as a swing on the dance card—and the fact that some women refused to dance with him for this fact—are suggestive of the myriad ways in which regulations and classification systems are maintained in social contexts where the explicit rules and regulations of competitions are not in play. Pete was mindful of the consequences for not adhering to the standards, and so he cued me as to what he was about to do as a courtesy. Had I exhibited any signs that I was uncomfortable with dancing "against the grain," I am confident he would not have done so. Although a rarity at the Regent for his interest in bucking convention, Pete's exception proves the rule. Most dancers welcomed the systems and standards and were not comfortable being left to their own devices.[1]

Ballroom dance features elaborate classificatory systems that regulate dance genres, steps, styles, and detailed formulae for prescribing movement.[2] Knowledge of these conventions is gained through extensive study by advanced dancers and professionals who have invested considerable time educating themselves on the theory of ballroom dance. These dancers act as guardians of correct performance and define conformity as beautiful while disdaining nonconformity as rough or excessive. The guardians pass on this knowledge to amateurs through formal and informal channels, and they exact consequences on those individuals who violate the regulations for performances that are perceived to be more immediately gratifying but less technically proficient or sophisticated. These guardians are legitimated through official and informal organizations that distribute titles, ranks, and rankings such as president, treasurer, professional, amateur, teacher, student, social dancer, competitor (including a range of competition titles and placements), and so forth.[3]

The regulations, conventions, and classifications common to ballroom inform performance. Dictating the ways bodies move, regulations provide a sense of predictability and safety for ballroom participants, as discussed in chapter 2, while they also provide a framework within which dancers understand the value and beauty of their movement and their bodies. Like all practices of symbolic distinction (Bourdieu 1984), the categories are simultaneously conceptual, social, and material, embodied by the dancers themselves and legitimized by their ubiquity in dance contexts.

This chapter serves two purposes. The first is to provide a basic introduction to the tenets of ballroom dance through the various classification systems social dancers used. Elementary lessons in ballroom dance functioned as a catechism into these various systems and their meaning, and so all ballroom dance experiences were shaped by these cognitive and cultural frameworks. In addition to laying out some preliminary groundwork on the genre, I suggest that these dance classifications are simultaneously social classifications that serve to stratify individuals and groups according to their perception of the social order. In this framework, classification struggles become a site for class struggles, for they dictate a sense of place in the social order and thereby fulfill the social processes of inclusion and exclusion. They are important because class struggle occurs not only over valued resources or for access to positions of power. The very definition of what is valued—and relatedly, what is beautiful—and the understanding of one's position within this social field are themselves the objects of struggle.

As a middlebrow leisure activity, ballroom dance is caught between the high and low within the larger stratification of American dance styles. Many couple-dance traditions performed in the United States have strong connections to lower-class communities. The range of southern two-step styles, Cajun, Texas, and country, for example, celebrate their deep connection, past and present, with America's white, rural working class. Others, such as swing, salsa, and tango, have experienced some upward mobility, but still trade on their roots in disenfranchised minority communities in the United States and elsewhere. On the other end of the spectrum are presentational, art-dance traditions such as ballet and modern, which signify European high society and U.S. elites. Over the last century ballroom proponents have navigated this terrain in a number of ways, rhetorically moving between elitism and populism, art and sport, presentational theater and participatory leisure, virtue and vice, depending on changing social contexts in order to stake a legitimate claim for ballroom performance among white, middle- and upper-middle-class dancers (Cook 1998; Wagner 1997).

In this way ballroom dance affinity groups have the potential to function as Weberian "status groups" or Bourdieu's "classes," which, the latter argues, are shaped by objective conditions, the product of a configuration of capital types including a range of symbolic dimensions. Class, therefore, cannot be quantified or reduced solely to economic figures. In fact, class is often defined as much by its "being-perceived as by its being" (Bourdieu 1984, 483). "Class identity is itself a matter of perception and conception as well as being materially constituted" (Swartz 1997, 148). The symbolic dimensions of class struggle, however, remain less studied than the more evident economic and material dimensions. Ballroom performance is constitutive and generative of class disposition, and it serves as a symbolic dimension of class struggle for middle-class dancers seeking to perform a unique style of rationalized (and thus classified and class-based) human movement.[4]

To this end, I approach the classification systems of ballroom dancing as a means for articulating the "legitimate vision of the social world and its division" (Swartz 1997, 147) according to this particular group of middle-class, midwestern ballroom dancers, who have attempted to distinguish ballroom from lower-class couple dance traditions and to align it with European classical forms. In particular, I have identified four themes that emerge from these classificatory systems, four discreet but interrelated sets of values that ballroom dancers understand to be linked to upper-class sensibilities, practice, and ideology: an emphasis on a high degree of specialization in performance; the demonstration of control over the body and its movement; the rationalization of movement and the ideas articulated by it, especially as mediated by language and other symbols; and an association with Western Europe. These values served to define a beautiful performance within a particular class-based sensibility that privilege those expressed in the presentational art forms of Western Europe. Through the various classification systems employed under the ballroom umbrella and described below, these values are enacted and manifest, structuring bodies, movement, and sensory experience for ballroom dancers. Performing these values within a couple-dance genre position, ballroom dancers hold a distinctive place in the world of American dance and communicate their particular class position as being betwixt and between, as middle-class Americans distinctly are (Bourdieu 1984; Morin 2008).[5]

I use the concept of rationalization here in both the colloquial sense of dancers justifying and explaining the choices they made as well as the definition more often used in social sciences that indicates the primacy given to logical and calculated decision-making apparatuses over more traditional or emotional (and presumably less systematic or efficient) value systems. In the early decades of the twentieth century, and even before, the rationalization of movement was an important strategy for wresting ballroom from the fray of lower-class social dances and aligning it with upper-class values. Whether the logic was based on high-art values of control, line, and sophistication; or medicine and sport science; or commercial success, it was (and still is) important for dancers to know that ballroom is understood (by themselves and their wider community) as being driven by universal principles accepted by American middle- and upper-class society rather than in the service of bodily pleasure or emotional states (Foster 1995, 1996; Tomko 1999; Wagner 1997).

Juliet McMains (2006) and Edward Myers (1984) suggest that the codification of ballroom on the part of the U.S. ballroom dance industry was a means for ensuring its economic viability. Eliminating improvisation and therefore eliding the distinctions between social, theatrical, and competitive practice was, McMains argues, "necessary for the economic viability of the ballroom dance industry, a strategic marketing tool utilized at least since the 1910s" to codify the genre into a "saleable product" of dance instruction (64). I would add to this argument that the industry was only successful in this tactic because the notion of increased control and rationalization of the body and its movement was aligned with the class disposition of U.S. ballroom dancers. In fact, rather than being a strategy thrust upon dancers for the economic viability of the industry, the gesture might best be perceived as a choice made by the dancers themselves—as dancers, consumers, and leaders of dance organizations—in order to symbolically lay claim to a particular class position by virtue of the literal control over the body that ballroom promoted.

In this light, and in light of the many claims about ballroom's connections to middle- and upper-class sensibilities (Cook 1998; Malnig 1997; McMains 2006; Myers 1984), I would urge caution in the temptation to reduce the middle-class dispositions performed in ballroom to an exercise of social dominance alone. This chapter suggests that while the act of performing ballroom dance is an articulation of a particular middle-class position, and that position is one of power in relation to the majority of the world's populations, it is also one of having less than (and perhaps being and feeling less than) the haute bourgeoisie on the opposite end of the metaphorical social ladder with whom the middle classes are more likely to identify. The undertones of fear and frustration at the betwixt-and-between-ness that mark the stories dancers told me about their experiences suggest that performing class is not always about performing power, or at least not always *only* about performing power. In the case of the Regent dancers, there was also a degree of working through doubt, fear, and feelings of disempowerment, also a product of being middle class, that were simultaneously at play. And finally, in the quotidian reality of moving through the world, it is also about the desire to be recognized as beautiful by those with the power to define it. Through the rationalized systems for classifying performance described below, dancers articulated a vision for the social world and their place in it, one accompanied by contradictory experiences of privilege and inferiority.

The Ballroom Umbrella

Referencing a Russian folktale, Mark Slobin (2000) likens klezmer music to a magical mushroom providing shelter, if not intoxication, to numerous and diverse musical refugees. Although klezmer is most widely recognized as a heritage tradition, Slobin states that "under the klezmer umbrella" lie many types of musicians and styles of performance that reflect "the power of American music to recombine and redefine itself" (3–4). Similarly, the large umbrella of ballroom performance encompasses a variety of dance and music traditions, styles, and steps with ethnically, geographically, and temporally diverse origins that are ordered within multiple, embedded, and overlapping classification systems. The overview of the most salient of these systems offered below is most deeply informed by my fieldwork within a particular local context of social ballroom dancers in the midwestern United States, but it takes into account practices common throughout the country and will have some resonance for various international contexts as well.

DANCESPORT AND SOCIAL DANCING

One of the major distinctions within ballroom performance is the line that is drawn between competitive practice and social dancing. Competitive ballroom dancing practices have increasingly become known by the term "DanceSport" (or, generically, "dancesport") in the United States and abroad; however, in my experience, the term was not used frequently in central Illinois. Instead, "competition" was the general gloss for what many competitors might call "dancesport." Competition ballroom combines athleticism, theater and spectacle, art and expressivity within the drama of elimination contests, prizes, and international prestige. Such contests have aired on television for years and have been the subject of numerous feature films (such as the American and Japanese versions of *Shall We Dance?*, *Dance with Me*, and *Strictly Ballroom*). Competitive practices are widely known today through a number of recent and highly successful reality television shows (such as the aforementioned *Dancing with the Stars* and *So You Think You Can Dance?*).

Competition ballroom is, by and large, a "presentational" form (Turino 2008), focusing on rehearsed, pre-choreographed routines and no partner exchange. Hallmarks of the style include extraordinary choreographic virtuosity, as defined by a high degree of physical control over all muscle groups and a concern for visual line and stylized expression. Couples perform in "heats" (note the sport terminology) with several other couples of similar capability, both for judges and for enthusiastic audience members, who shout words of encouragement over the music. As such, these competitions (of which there are "championships," "cups," and "games," among many others) are unique events, reminiscent of both sporting events and classical dance concerts. Preparing amateur students for such international, regional, and collegiate events is the bread and butter of many dance studios, and this is especially true of franchised organizations such as the Fred Astaire and Arthur Murray Studios.[6]

Competition dancing is a world unto itself, with a range of formal organizations and institutions that govern performance, pedagogy, and commerce. The twentieth century was marked by the proliferation and jostling of formal organizations as they transitioned from independent regional bodies to national and now international and "worldwide" organizations in the business of governing ballroom dance. At all levels, these organizations are typically led by "insiders," holding rank and title, and are driven by a desire to promote dancing, most explicitly (but not solely) as an Olympic-worthy athletic and competitive practice (dancesport) (McMains 2006).

The World DanceSport Federation (WDSF), known until 2011 as the International DanceSport Federation (IDSF), is recognized by the International Olympic Committee as the worldwide governing body for dancesport and wheelchair dancesport. The IDSF was founded in 1957 under a different name, International Council of Amateur Dancers, which it held until 1990, when formal ballroom dance competition organizations heightened efforts in their ongoing campaign for Olympic-sport status (Braun 1996). The WDSF hosts "national members," the national-level affiliate organizations that report to the WDSF. For instance, USA Dance, formerly known as USABDA (the United States Amateur Ballroom Dancers Association, Inc.), is the national governing body for dancesport in the United States, with more than 150 regional chapters nationwide supporting both social and competitive ballroom dancing. Their informational materials state that the organization was founded with the mission of establishing ballroom dance as an Olympic sport and also that about 70 percent of USA Dance members are recreational ballroom dancers. "For most dancers, it's about having fun, making new friends, and staying fit. For the athlete, it's also the competitive experience" (http://usadance.org, accessed September 3, 2012).

USA Dance, in turn, hosts smaller, regional organizations, including collegiate groups. Many major universities and smaller colleges have formal ballroom dance clubs. The University of Illinois at Urbana-Champaign sponsors the Dancing Illini, a formally constituted student club with officers, a sizable budget, a curriculum of dance class offerings and weekly practice sessions. The Dancing Illini hosts an annual intercollegiate dance competition on campus every fall .[7]

USA Dance is but one of ninety-two national member bodies hosted by the WDSF, who reported that their membership quadrupled between 1970 and 2010. Others include, for example, Dancesport Scotland, DanceSport Federation of Serbia, Fédération Camerounaise Des Danses Sportives et Assimilé (DanceSport Federation of Cameroon), and the Zimbabwe Amateur DanceSport Association. As of 1995, the WDSF also hosts Associate Memberships for other dance organizations, such as the World Rock 'n' Roll Confederation, the United Country and Western Dance Council, and the World Baton Twirling Federation.

Another important organization for competition is the Imperial Society for Teachers of Dancing (ISTD). A London-based organization for dance teachers, the ISTD provides training, curricula, and examination boards to teachers and examiners across a range of dance styles, including ballroom. The WDSF uses the ballroom technique books published by the ISTD in the formation of its restricted syllabus—the steps used in competition dance. In developing his own curriculum for the Regent, David Lin referred to the ISTD dance technique books and required students in his dance theory class to purchase the set.

For dancesport competitors in particular, these organizations are the important accrediting body for the world ranking of competitors, authorizing the set of moves for competitive practice (the restricted syllabus), sanctioning nonregulation dancesport performance, and various other practices and policies that uphold the orthodoxy of competitive ballroom performance. Dancesport organizations also represent the interests of competitive dancers to the International Olympic Committee.

Ballroom performance, however, does exist outside the purview of the WDSF and even the national membership bodies. Known simply as "social dancing," a term used to distinguish this style from "competition dancing," social dancing coexists alongside competition as a casual and occasional opportunity for nonspecialist, noncompeting dancers to have fun, interact, and dance within a participatory context (Turino 2008). Social dancers may spend a great deal of time dancing but do so within the context of an evening of socializing with friends rather than developing technique for placing in formal competition. This is not to say that social dancers do not also work on technique and improving their performance, but usually they do so within and for social dance contexts rather than for placing in competitions.

Venues for social ballroom dance are plentiful but more ad hoc and less standardized in nature. One need not be accredited to run a private studio or offer classes through any number of civic organizations, such as community centers, colleges and universities, park districts, and the like. It is entirely up to the dance instructor as to the degree to which they will adhere (or not) to dancesport federation guidelines and practices.

Social dancers occasionally participate in local dance competitions, but generally the focus of their performance is to have fun within a participatory context, minus the judges, cameras, and viewing audience common to competition venues. As David repeated to me on numerous occasions, "If my students stop having fun, they quit. They want to get better, sure, but it always has to be fun first." Unlike competition studios that rely on placement in competitions to reinforce the economic value of the investment of time and money learning to dance, David's model relies on pleasure as the explicit motivator for bringing them back week after week.[8]

Social and competitive dancing are simultaneously distinct and deeply entwined, and they continually feed into and off of one another.[9] Given the pervasive influence of competition and theatrical exhibition dancing more generally, social ballroom dance lies in a unique place on the spectrum of performance practices (Turino 2008; Penny 1999). It is public performance, somewhat presentational within a collective and participatory ethos, but it is also an intimate, private act between two people. It is part dramatic theater and part unreflected-upon reality.

Among both types of dancers, competitors are recognized as the more knowledgeable and accomplished performers. Today they serve as inspiration for social performers just as the famous husband-and-wife dancing partnership of Vernon and Irene Castle as well as Fred Astaire and Ginger Rogers did for dancers decades ago. In this way, extreme technical virtuosity and precision, and the methods by which they are achieved, are celebrated as the most prestigious and valued type of performance, and they fuel the self-imaginary with images by which social dancers understand their own embodied experience. In return, social dancers ground competitive practice in everyday social life and social relationships—husband and wives, fathers and daughters, young (heterosexual) lovers—providing narrative fodder for the highly stylized "representations of social dance" competitors perform for screaming audiences on the competition circuit (McMain 2006, 65).[10]

The stylized and theatrical nature of presentational performance dominates in competitive and exhibition performance, and even when competitors seek opportunities to ground their performance in the evocation of authentic heteronormative love relationships that more commonly typify social dancing, the extreme costumes and stylized performance also signal to viewers that this is spectacle, and characters are being portrayed.[11] Both styles of performance, competition and social, provide a conceptual and comparative framework for understanding the other, entwining a valuation of virtuosic specialization with the narrative drama of everyday human social relationships.

As action, drama, and spectacle, social ballroom dancing invites the performer to step outside of his or her habits and to step into new roles and try on different characters. However, dancers and audience members also perceive the performance as an authentic representation of the self. The experience of being simultaneously self and other is symbolically rich, stimulating the imagining of what is and what is possible (Deloria 1998; Desmond 1997; Skinner 2008; Turino 1999; Turino and Lea 2004). This type of performance exists outside the norms of everyday life yet has real ramifications for the lives of its performers.

In her description of early-twentieth-century social ballroom dancing in American cabarets, Linda Tomko notes that amateur social dancers took the floor initially inhabited by their professional, exhibition counterparts. "Patrons themselves thus became the subjects for examination, evaluation, and possibly emulation by other observing diners. Slipping from viewer to doer, patrons tasted the difference between passive and active seeking of pleasure in bodily motion and the shifts in kinesthetic awareness that must have accompanied such a translation from audience to performer" (1999, 27). Moreover, I would suggest that social dancers engage multiple subject positions simultaneously. While they routinely move from a seat in the audience to a position on the floor, both ways of knowing dance—as a visual spectacle and a physical sensation—fuse. The experience of one informs the other.[12] When moving, dancers are simultaneously interpreting their performance as an authentic, participatory sensation and as something to be viewed and evaluated. Many dancers can be seen checking themselves in the mirrors that line the walls of the Regent and watching others watch them as they move down the line of dance. One Regent dancer states, "I'm simply the most happy and content when I'm dancing—watching others dance would run a close second." While not the same phenomenon, moving and watching movement exist together in a reciprocal relationship experientially and cognitively. Competition and social dancing both feature this experience of action and spectacle but discursively and kinesthetically reinforce different elements of this experience.

The recent campaign for Olympic status on the part of dancesport (competition) ballroom dance organizations is but one stage in a long-term effort not only to promote but also to legitimate the genre—particularly necessary in earlier decades when social dance came under fire from the anti-dance movement, driven by puritanical beliefs about the dangers of dance, especially its performance in social contexts. In the face of this resistance, dance proponents exercised a number of strategies to justify and promote performance among average citizens and their children (see Tomko 1999; Wagner 1997). Prior to the twentieth century, dance masters equated social dancing with high art, framing dance as an ennobling activity akin to classical arts and emphasizing the shared movement vocabulary with ballet (Aldrich 1991; McMains 2006; Tomko 1999). At the start of the twentieth century, dancers augmented this position by also suggesting that dance was not only mentally and morally edifying, but it was also physically healthy as well, drawing strength from the increased importance physical exercise was granted in modern medicine. Drawing upon modernity's increasing turns toward rationalization, the body gradually fell under the auspices of medical and sport science as well as artistic criticism as another object to be controlled. Simultaneously, the discourse of leisure, a result of labor reform in the early 1900s, also broadened the popularity of public, social dancing beyond elite circles and private salons to middle-class America (Tomko 1999; Wagner 1997).

The discourses—dance as art, sport, and leisure—have been a part of ballroom parlance ever since, informing the distinction between competitive and social dance practice. They reinforce one another as well, as the emphasis on muscle control is legitimated by the value of elegant line and graceful movement to the end of having fun and becoming more healthful—values articulated both in the explicit judging of competitors and the informal evaluation of social dancers alike.

At the Regent, where there were but three and occasionally four national-level competitors in regular attendance, social dancers combined these three discourses in a particular way, as exemplified by the story that Mai and Dan use to explain why they dance. To paraphrase, "We are older, no kids to take care of, work is going well. . . . We had free time and wanted to do something together. Dan's doctor suggested that he try dancing or something like it to get moving, you know, for his health. Ballroom is so elegant, the classical music so beautiful, and it turned out to be so much fun, so it was an easy choice for us." Ballroom dance presented the couple with benefits in terms of leisure time, physical health, and artistry.

The rest of this book is invested in describing social dance practice, presenting an ethnographically grounded study of social ballroom dance as performed by amateur hobbyists of various skill levels and providing a complement to the more plentiful academic and trade-publication scholarship on competitive practice (see, for example, Erickson 2011; Marion 2008; Malnig 1992, 2009; Marceau 1998; McMains 2006; Penny 1997, 1999; and Picart 2006). It will describe the pedagogy and style of social dance performance and detail the ways social dancers conceived of their performance, taking as its example the local dance community in central Illinois, presenting a side of ballroom dance that is at once more typical and still less exposed than the more visible and spectacular competition ballroom dance.

The recent proliferation of research into the social worlds of competitive dancing has been incredibly valuable in documenting the social styles and aesthetic values and practices of these unique and important dance cultures. However, the ubiquity of these sources has perhaps had the unintended effect of creating an "orthodoxy" of ballroom dance practices that are almost entirely based on the rather unique values of dancesport organizations. In fact, the discursive practices of these organizations tend to reinforce this orthodoxy, as they attempt to brand their particular vision of ballroom dancing as a universal norm. This convergence of discourses—academic and popular media that document the aesthetic values and practices of competitive ballroom dance cultures, and dancesport institutions that sell their particular brand of dancing as both "official" and "universal"—has created a situation wherein all other forms of noncompetitive ballroom dance practices are often understood as somehow "anomalous." To the contrary, there are myriad ballroom dance communities that exist and thrive outside the hegemony of the competitive dance world (or worlds), and they must be understood on their own terms and not simply as "aspiring competitors." The dance community in Savoy is one such example, and it would be both an injustice to the dancers in this community and simply analytically erroneous to gloss their dance practices as "incorrect" or "immature" versions of competitive dance practices. Rather, this community exists alongside the competitive dance communities—sometimes in conversation with, sometimes working against, sometimes completely ignoring the world of competitive dance.

INTERNATIONAL AND AMERICAN STYLES

Over the last century, two categories have emerged, American and International, that reference two slightly different styles of ballroom performance. The American style developed primarily in the United States and is occasionally portrayed as a simplified version of the International style, which originated in Western Europe.

The features that distinguish the two styles vary with genre. For instance, International foxtrot uses a completely different basic step from American foxtrot; the same is true of tango, rumba, and waltz. In other genres the essential footwork patterns are the same, but there are differences in stylistic features such as the motion of the knees and hand gestures. At the Regent, dancers performed International or American style as they preferred, to the same musical example. In competition contexts, different music with subtle variation in tempo and style is tailored to whether the event features International or American style.[13] In larger dancesport events, both styles are performed in separate heats. In smaller, regional events, including the local collegiate competition, both International and American dancers perform simultaneously to the same musical example in the same heat.

American style was the default for group classes at the Regent, but David also offered upper-level classes and individual lessons on International style, generally for those interested in competing. The reservation of International style for advanced levels of instruction caused some local dancers to perceive the International style as more difficult and prestigious. The prestige of the International style is also rooted in its associations with Western Europe (namely England), the perceived sophistication of European cultural practices, and the perception that International style carried greater value in competitions.

For instance, retired amateur competitor William discusses the demands of competition International tango after having performed social American tango at the Regent for more than a year since retiring. In his comments, we hear the eliding of beginners with American and advanced dancers with competition and International style:

> Tango is such a different beast than everything else. And you really have to—well, at this stage, to make tango feel right—you really have to have a good partner, because I'm used to so much response from my partner. And beginners just don't, they have no clue how to be on their feet enough, in the right balance so that they can make their bodies respond that way. And I haven't done International tango seriously in a year now. So I dance with [my former competition partner] the other night [and] it was like aaaaah [takes his imaginary partner in his arms], this is odd.

In this context, the tango about which William speaks is less connected with Argentina and more so about the more demanding (and thus more prestigious) International style of ballroom dance. The informal prestige granted to the International style was but one way that dancers created connections between their performance and the perceived sophistication of Western Europe.

The continued maintenance of the American and International ballroom categories is one of the ways a particular middle-class American imaginary was constructed. In this worldview, America is distinct from but less sophisticated than its European counterparts. As in many other contexts of ballroom parlance, the rhetoric here functions simultaneously as an articulation of social power and of disenfranchisement. One important element for the dancers I worked with was the fact that they were located in a small, rural, midwestern town set in the middle of corn and soybean fields hours from any metropolitan area. Elite values are typically grounded in urbanity, and while my informants were elites in a local, small-town context, they also understood their residence in rural America as a liability that cost them cultural capital on a national front. Frequent references to international travel, the acquisition of goods only commonly found in urban centers, and disparaging remarks about the parochial nature of central Illinois helped individuals to distance themselves from the provincialism commonly perceived to be part of the rural American experience. My interactions with Regent dancers often involved a discussion of recently acquired luxury goods that served to articulate a particular socioeconomic class in order to distinguish themselves from local, lower-class rural sensibilities. For instance, one Regent dancer began an interview with me by discussing the luxury dual drawer dishwashers he was planning to use in his kitchen remodel.

> That's the beauty of these real cool dishwashers. You know little things make it, umm, [pause] actually I don't know, I just cannot imagine regular people would spend this kind of money.

Similarly, the Regent sponsored an annual cruise, each year traveling farther afield than the last. During the early years of my research, trips were to the typical Caribbean destinations, then later to Alaska and West Coast, and then to international locales, such as Peru and China in the last years of my residence. Dozens of dancers make this trip yearly, and they return to tell stories of dancing and sightseeing in these most "exotic" and beautiful places. Both David and Ellen Lin are avid photographers, taking thousands of pictures during each trip, culling them to the best selections, and sharing them publicly by dressing the Regent lobby bulletin boards and website. Photos of friends and fellow dancers atop Machu Picchu or posing on a busy Shanghai street testify to the worldliness of cruise participants, celebrating the communities created through shared travel experiences and enticing new dancers to join them on the next trip. Cruises have an added benefit in that they routinely feature ballroom performance and are one of the few social venues outside of studios to do so. Through cruising, ballroom dancers can affirm the worth of their investment in performance by their ability to dance literally around the world.

References to extensive travel, luxury goods, and urban values all function as a way to stake claims to a more cosmopolitan, and thus higher-class disposition than local elites could otherwise make. They also give voice to the importance of the distance traveled, literal and cultural, which is required in order to successfully stake such claims and assuage any feelings of insecurity about the right to make them on the grounds of local conditions alone.[14]

GENRE HIERARCHY AND PRESTIGE

Just as individual dancers are qualified, the dance genres themselves are characterized and classified along a range of criteria. As previous work has demonstrated, "genre worlds" (Holt 2007; Negus 1996, 1999) are powerful expressions of collective cultural knowledge, and as such they help social groups to generate affinity and to articulate difference one from another. Genres are, in a sense, rhetorical actions with social consequences (Harris 1995; Miller 1984). The Regent ballroom dancers, like many ballroomers around the world, juggle anywhere from four to twenty-plus genres in their practice. As such, the ways

Table 1: Hierarchical valuation of partnership dances.

Competition Ballroom Dances		***Social Ballroom Dances***
International Style Standard or Modern	*International Style Latin*	*Street/Club*
American Style Smooth	*American Style Rhythm*	
Waltz	(Paso doble)	West Coast swing
Viennese waltz	Rhumba/Bolero	Hustle
Tango	Cha Cha	Mambo
Foxtrot	Samba	Nightclub two-step
Quickstep	Jive/East Coast swing	Salsa
	Merengue	

Note: Dances are in descending order of level of perceived sophistication within their respective subcategories. Subcategories are ordered left to right by perceived level of sophistication.

in which they define and order genres reveals something of what it means to become beautiful.

Table 1 presents my own abstraction of the classification system that Regent dancers used to order the various genres they performed. To condense a complicated discourse into a small chart in this manner runs the risk of suggesting that the ideas contained within it are fixed rather than the rich, contextually specific, and malleable network of actions and ideas that it is. I do not suggest that the genre worlds within which social ballroom dancers operate are static; rather, I wish to to show how various beliefs, especially with regard to value and beauty, are articulated through the actions and discourses required to maintain a classification system of dance genres that fall under the ballroom umbrella. What I have provided is most deeply informed by my years of fieldwork with Regent dancers, which itself is informed in sporadic ways by the national and international (as well as virtual and face-to-face) networks of social and competition dance. Other ballroom dance contexts will yield a slightly (or perhaps radically) different chart, though I would contend that all ballroom contexts are marked by a similar kind of discursive engagement in the hierarchical distinction of the various genres ballroom dancers perform.[15]

The ideas contained within Table 1 were articulated in myriad ways by Regent dancers. In classes, teachers made them explicit in lessons as well as in the printed materials distributed in the class. In private lessons as well as in private and casual conversations, the ideas were developed further—especially in terms of relative prestige, elegance, and complexity. Social dance events that feature printed dance cards and a deejay also reinforced the generic categorization of musical examples to movement.

At the Regent, the largest categorical generic distinction existed between competition and social dance genres, which reinforced the divide discussed above between competition and social dancers. Competition genres were those required in typical formal competitions (though they could be performed in social contexts by social dancers) and social ballroom genres, or noncompetition dances that were not believed to be central to the ballroom competition syllabus and were believed to be less standardized and global. The competition dances formed the heart of the ballroom repertory, whereas the social dances (most often called "nightclub" or "street dances" at the Regent) were considered peripheral to the standard canon and were, in fact, typically less standardized within ballroom contexts (see Appendix for brief descriptions of each genre listed in this chart).

The competition dances were then further subdivided into two categories that use different names with regard to whether they reference the American or International style. According to dancesport guidelines, the group containing the waltz, foxtrot, Viennese waltz, tango, and quickstep is called "Smooth" in American style, and "Standard" in International style. Officially, the term Standard replaced its predecessor, "Modern," decades ago, but Regent dancers used the two in equal measure. The second category of competition dances, which includes the rhumba or bolero, cha cha, samba, jive, East Coast swing, and the paso doble, is called "Rhythm" in the American style and "Latin" in the International style.

While the terms Modern, Smooth, and Standard are used in very particular ways by competitors to indicate International or American styles of performance and particular historical moments, Regent dancers were not as invested in the official terminology and used the terms interchangeably. For instance, while Regent dancers most often performed in the American style, they generally used the labels associated with International style, and so I will do the same, understanding that it presents a contradiction to standard competitive practice.

Together, the competition genres form the heart of the ballroom repertory. They are highly standardized for their use in competitions, as well as for pedagogical purposes, and function as powerful structuring concepts even among social dancers. In chapter 5 I will provide a microanalysis of these two categories with specific regard to how they articulate ideas about race within this class-based value system, but I will introduce them briefly here.

The Standard dances (waltz, Viennese waltz, tango, foxtrot, and quickstep) are all traveling dances, meaning that the couple travels counterclockwise around the dance floor in closed position and makes limited use of open position.[16] For the most part, the Standard dances are the oldest genres in the repertory, are derived from European origins, and are considered the "classic" styles by ballroom dancers. For instance, Kelly, a middle-aged saleswoman and mother of two adult children, said she began dancing to learn social graces, enjoys ballroom for "the control of different muscle groups," and prefers the waltz because she "studied the Western classical music." Like many of her peers, Kelly compressed the social comportment of upper-class society, control of the body, and western European art traditions together into one aesthetic experience through performance of the waltz, considered the "crown jewel" of ballroom dance.

The Latin category (paso doble, rhumba, rumba, cha cha, samba, jive and East Coast swing)[17] includes spot dances: the couple does not travel around but remains basically fixed at one point, or spot, on the floor. They also contain many steps in open position. The majority of Latin dances have origins in Latin America, but swing is an African-American dance, while paso doble is from Spain. The paso doble holds a unique position in that it is rarely performed in any context other than competition, and in fact, it was never performed socially at the Regent during my time there.[18]

The third category of ballroom dances, Nightclub, is standardized to a much lesser degree. By virtue of this fact it is more often subject to locally specific values and practices than the others and thus more highly variable from one site to another and is valued the least. During my tenure at the Regent, these dances included the Nightclub two-step (not related to the country or Texas two-step), hustle, West Coast swing, and in the most recent years salsa, merengue, and (on rare occasion) bachata. Nightclub dances are those that are currently popular in nightclub settings, have their recent history in nightclubs, or can translate easily into the context of a nightclub; the dancers at my fieldsite colloquially called them the "street dances." They generally do not constitute formal competition categories on the ballroom circuit unless the competition features a "nightclub" heat (this is not standard practice but may occur in regional contexts). Nightclub dances are often performed during the intermissions of formal organized ballroom events and as such may not actually appear in the program of events. The cottage industry of ballroom dance music does produce some recordings of songs specifically for the performance of these genres within ballroom dance contexts, but at my fieldsite it was common for ballroom dance deejays to bypass this option and instead cull their selections from popular radio hits.

Dancers valued the Nightclub genres the least and were often quick to qualify such dances as possessing potential but lacking in some way. They typically suggested that the Nightclub genres were in need of stylistic elevation in order to be on par with ballroom in terms of sophistication and occasionally undertook the enterprise as well. For instance, during my fieldwork, the University of Illinois Latin American student club hosted a night of Latin dancing with a live band in the University Union. The organizers planned a number of dance competitions and solicited judges from ballroom studios.[19] I was one such judge. During the bachata competition, two of the ballroom judges used their authority to "correct" one element of bachata performance they found particularly problematic. "We cannot place any couple if any of their feet leave the ground," one judge demanded, referring to the hip check at the end of the bachata basic that can occasionally lead to the woman's back foot being lifted off the floor, a common trait of the genre as performed by Dominicans.

At the time Bachata was only recently becoming familiar to ballroom dancers, and while they recognized a kinship between bachata and the Latin dances they loved and performed, they found the style as performed by Dominicans at salsa clubs to be too sexualized. My fellow judge and ballroom dancer was using this opportunity to create what he believed to be a more sophisticated style of bachata in which all the dancers held their own weight (an important element in ballroom) and eliminated what he interpreted as the sexualized "grinding" that could occur between partners at the end of the basic step. My protests that this was a particularly important signifier of regional style, especially for Dominican dancers who feel a sense of ownership over the genre, fell on deaf ears. The result was that the Dominican dancers were eliminated in the first round. Controversy was sparked when a couple of Middle Eastern novice dancers who had recently learned bachata through a Dancing Illini class were declared the winners. The winners were perhaps the most surprised of all.

When I asked ballroom dancers about performers of Nightclub genres, I often received comments such as, "They just keep doing the same few moves over and over again," or "It's so chaotic. They are not in control of their own bodies." One dancer likened salsa to vertical sex.[20] They also characterized the contexts in which these genres are performed as being problematic for the prevalence of alcohol and a highly sexualized "meat market" mentality.

Within the respective categories there exists a less formal and less explicit ranking of the individual genres according to a number of factors that is most reducible to the degree to which the genre is considered sophisticated. This is measured by a complicated formula that includes the type of movement, the style of accompanying music, and the country of origin, all of which are contextualized within a particular historical trajectory that can strongly influence and perhaps override these elements. For example, the amount of time a genre has existed in the ballroom repertory significantly informs its location within the repertory's hierarchical organization. Table 1 presents the dominant shared viewpoint on the relative value of the various genres, but in fact this aspect of hierarchy is more individualized and context specific.

Table 1 presents a snapshot of a particular local context, yet genres can and have moved within the canonical hierarchy through time, and the categories themselves have shifted over the last one hundred years. It is not at all as fixed as this kind of chart would make it seem. Historically, most of the genres in this canon, such as waltz, tango, rumba, and foxtrot, began as the equivalent of "street" dances and have risen to a position of prestige and respectability through a process of stylistic transformation (Bosse 1999, 2004) and standardization. These prestigious genres have served as models for the "development" of other dances that currently place lower in the canon.

Regardless of where they originated, contemporary practice finds the oldest genres in the Standard category, whereas the newest additions are found in the Nightclub category. Thus, while it may seem to defy categorical logic, ballroom-style tango, one of the oldest genres in the repertory, is not classified in the category of Latin dances but rather in that of Standard.

As one of the oldest genres in the repertory, ballroom-style tango has been subject to stylistic modification according to the preferences of ballroom dancers and currently is more stylistically aligned with the waltz than with the style of tango currently (or likely ever) performed in Argentina. Hence, ballroom dancers know and perform three different styles of tango: the American and International ballroom styles as well as Argentine tango, which was generally treated as a nightclub dance. Generally speaking, the tango and its companions in the Modern category are more standardized and codified than the other types of dances and thus are perceived to embody the cultural and aesthetic values of the ballroom community to the highest degree.

Above all, ballroom dancers value beauty, grace, and precision. All of these depend on virtuosic degrees of physical control over every muscle group, and ballroom dancers spend much of their practice time learning to control the muscle groups required to perform dance steps correctly. Ideal execution of the Standard dances demands more physical control relative to their Nightclub counterparts, and one of the main criticisms ballroom dancers wage at nonballroom genres is that nightclub dancers are stylistically uncontrolled and undisciplined, which is occasionally interpreted as an iconic representation of their lack of control and discipline in the social realm.

The Standard dances such as waltz and foxtrot are considered the most complex because their ideal performance looks effortless. The audience should not be made aware of how much effort is being expended and how much control is being commanded; rather it should perceive a floating, graceful couple for whom such polish is a natural outward expression of interior refinement. On the other hand, sweat and physical exertion are not necessarily inappropriate in the performance of the less "classic" Latin dances. Rather than graceful, these genres are perceived as energetic, lively, and sexy—but authentic (see chapter 5 for more on the social value of the dance categories and Appendix for brief descriptions of each genre mentioned above).

The canon of ballroom genres is further solidified and perpetuated by the adoption of new genres and styles, which was itself motivated by changing notions of propriety and sexuality through the twentieth century. The development of ballroom dance and music has been fueled by the consistent appropriation of genres perceived to be lower class, attractive for their sexualized and racialized exotic character but in need of "domestication" for unqualified acceptance (see Bosse 1999). While the twentieth century experienced the rise and fall of many different couple dances, within the ballroom there remained some semblance of a core repertory, with the addition of one or two new dances approximately every ten years and with each new genre taking its place at the bottom of the hierarchical canon while pushing the others to the next highest position on the structure. This continuous influx of new genres enlivens and affirms the social investment in the hierarchical valuation of genres as it also stimulates a reorganization "from the bottom up."

DANCE STEPS

Just as contexts, people, and genres are grouped and categorized along rational and logical divisions, so too are the dance moves themselves (more often called steps) ordered accordingly. While not a salient category at the Regent, the notion of regulation dance steps (which begs another category, that of unregulated steps), spoofed to great effect in the Australian film *Strictly Ballroom*, was not an unfamiliar concept. For competition, ballroom dance moves are arranged in syllabi according to levels of difficulty, ranked bronze (beginning), silver (intermediate), and gold (most advanced). Although David's curriculum was his own innovation, it was informed by these categories, and he was keenly aware of how he had distributed various moves from these three categories across his curriculum.[21]

In David's pedagogy, the instructor first taught the basic rhythm and footwork, then introduced another slightly more difficult step, and then taught dancers to sequence the two together in what were called patterns. The curriculum for each class involved a series of named steps strung together to form a larger pattern sequence that could be repeated several times within one song. As the classes moved from novice to intermediate to advanced, the sequences became longer and employed more difficult moves.

A range of symbols was used to communicate knowledge about movement. The most immediately intuitive and comprehensible was the use of "slow" and "quick" to denote the rhythm of the step. The East Coast swing basic, for instance, was noted as "slow, slow, quick, quick" often abbreviated in text to "S,S,Q,Q." Certain moves, or sequences of moves, were codified with proper names, such as the "twinkle," "reverse twinkle," or "passing twinkle" in the American waltz.[22]

Regent Ballroom — **2nd Course**

SWING	WALTZ	RUMBA
(S,S,Q,Q,)	(1,2,3,)	(Q, Q, S)
1. In-out	1. Twinkle	1. Fallaway
2. Basic Turn Right	2. Left Turn	2. Cross Body Lead
3. Out W/U.A.T.	3. Left Side By Side	3. Alternating U.A.T.
4. U.A.T. W/Rt Hand		
5. Twin City	**FOXTROT**	**CHA CHA CHA**
6. Pretzel	(S,S,Q,Q)	(1,2,3,4 &)
	1. Running Steps	1. Basic
	2. ZigZag (Outside Partner)	2. Crossover Breaks
	3. Side Rocks	3. Underarm Turn
	4. Conversation W/U.A.T.	4. Chase

Figure 1: Facsimile of a handout featuring the Regent Ballroom course content for Ballroom Dance Class II. The class involves lessons in the five dances listed on the handout and lists the suggested way to count the basic step directly under the dance genre name, with *S* standing for "slow step" and *Q* standing for "quick step" to indicate the relative rhythmic values of the steps. Measuring steps with "slow" and "quick" was standard at the Regent and is common throughout the ballroom world.

Edward Myers argues that the creation of distinctions between movement patterns as indicated by proper names given to the steps is one way that dance was commodified: "Each component of a step pattern and every permutation and combination of them in the step manuals is named. Through this device, constituent differences among moves are signified, and each takes on an independent identity. Although treated as if they had the same concreteness as a can of peas, the dance steps are somewhat more elusive by nature" (1984, 76).

The dance steps as rationalized through symbolic representation and formal names, classificatory systems, and their transformation into commodities allow the movement of ballroom dancers to be valued differently in social terms. Grounding performance in rules and systems eliminates the concern of personal choice and the perceived danger that bodily desires and pleasure might influence movement choices, thereby distancing ballroom dance from solo club dancing and other types of couple dancing perceived to be authentic indicators of sexual desire.

On a rare occasion, as demand necessitated, David also offered a dance theory course that was quite demanding: it was offered twice during my seven years of fieldwork. This course was offered primarily for those interested in competing or becoming dance instructors. In this course, students studied the manuals from the International Society for Teachers of Dancing, which include the detailed syllabi for the bronze-, silver-, and gold-level steps. The dance notation in these manuals looks more like algebra than anything meant to notate movement, and it represents, in my mind at least, the most extreme rationalization of movement expressed in ballroom. This is not to devalue the role of notation for pedagogical purposes but simply to highlight the symbolic abstraction of dance as occurs in the development of any notation system.

At the Regent, visual notation was never used in group classes, where the instruction was more likely to rely on spoken metaphors and lessons from engineering and physics.[23] The leadership of the local ballroom dance scene was populated by engineering and science students, and this fact created a particular cultural tendency to consider dance in terms of physical laws. William discussed his experience teaching a class for the Dancing Illini:

> You know something like 90 percent of the guys were in the hard sciences and something like 80 percent of the women were. And every once in a while you'd find somebody from, you know, political science or some[thing]. They were the oddballs, just strange to see one of those. I mean, on Wednesday night or Thursday night when I'm teaching this class I asked how many people had taken physics class, you know. Everybody raised their hands. It was like, oh ok. Ha. Then I'll explain this in terms of isosceles triangles and force vectors. [Laughs]. This makes it easy.

Many of David's students told me they loved the "floating" quality of the waltz. David, who was one semester short of an engineering degree before dropping out to pursue his dance career, explained the phenomenon this way:

> The floating quality, . . . when most people refer to this, is if you're on a swing, the idea is that you have the highest velocity when you are at the bottom. Because you go *whooom* [he gestures the upward and forward momentum generated from the increase in velocity]. If you drag your feet on the sand, you will not go up as far. So what most dancers will do is that they will go down [on one], and grab the sand, [meaning] they pause for a moment, then they can't get up. They do not achieve body flight. So what most people enjoy, and they're trying to learn, is the trick of, when you say one, you're foot doesn't land there. But most dancers will do [as he slams his foot flat on the floor] *one*! They wanna land there—versus, for me, on one, I'm moving [as he demonstrates, moving through one].

The use of terms like velocity and force vectors, while likely not common parlance at all social dance studios, was typical in the classes and lessons I observed at the Regent and with the Dancing Illini, where the intellectually elite clientele was familiar with the abstraction of movement into scientific terms. The transference of the "human body in motion" into science's more general "objects in motion" was not only comfortable territory, it was preferred territory aligned with a worldview that privileges such laws to be artful in their reason. The logical breakdown of sequences to steps and then further into smaller movement units, all facilitated by a considerable use of language, appealed to the scientific mind, as William, a trained computer engineer, explained: "Well, if you think about the process of learning to dance, it's very process step-oriented, which is the sort of a thing you can imagine an engineer liking." Chad, a middle-aged technician of heating and cooling systems and Regent dancer, said he was "hooked on it from [the] beginning. It was like a math game, figuring out dance patterns." A medical student claimed, "Ballroom is a craft that has appealing precision." The scientific metaphors they employ elevate dancers' movement—and, by extension, dancers' bodies—to artful. Employing this "math-like" system, Regent dancers perform their appreciation for precision and logic, and they embody their conception of beauty as ordered and rational.

For hobbyists, this kind of rationalization of movement can be a comforting element. No mysterious artistic talent necessary. Just objects in motion, as Newton's laws explain. This refers to any body in motion, regardless of the shape, weight, and style of that body, or the degree of talent, beauty, grace, or prestige with which that body is attributed. That these laws are not discriminating, are open to all moving bodies, and result in an experience that is pleasing—physically, emotionally and aesthetically—is what makes ballroom dance ideal for those who choose to do it.

The classificatory systems reviewed here, including performance contexts, styles, genre, and movement, are but a few of the most salient ways that dancers abstracted movement, conceptualizing it in a more cognitively consumable system that reflected their own understanding of the social order. In presenting these regulations governing performance, especially as abstracted in charts and figures, I do not mean to suggest that they are static or fixed structures; rather, they are maintained, negotiated, and reshaped in practice. The assertion, maintenance, and contesting of aesthetic hierarchies and canon formation is a process that occurs in both explicit discourse as well as the tacit assumptions that equate beauty and prestige. The history of ballroom dance, as a genre that has existed for more than one hundred years, testifies to the processual nature of aesthetic classification systems and how the value of various types of performance by various types of bodies has shifted relatively according to historical context (Bosse 1999).

Together, these systems and the processes by which they are maintained articulate what beauty is by asserting and reinforcing a set of class-based principles that value an emphasis on a high degree of specialization in performance; the demonstration of control over the body and its movement; the rationalization of movement and the ideas articulated by it, especially as mediated by language and other symbols; and finally, an alignment with the aesthetic values of presentational artistic practice from Western Europe. These principles, as they have emerged over ballroom's history, have been employed at various moments to justify ballroom as a certain type of activity appropriate for middle-class Americans. They have allowed Americans to make claims about the legitimacy of the genre on the grounds that it is artistically beautiful and thus edifying on moral, intellectual, social, and physical grounds (see also Myers 1984).

Ballroom performance, with its emphasis on precision and extended formal training, requires substantial resources in terms of leisure time and money. Its performance articulates ballroom dancers' class position by the supposition of the considerable economic and cultural capital, and distance from necessity, it requires. A social function of ballroom dance is that it translates dancers' material conditions into symbolic distinctions (Bourdieu 1984). As such, ballroom was set apart from the lower-class dances that were readily available to individuals with little capital. That club dances can be learned "on the fly" during a night of dancing, at least by ballroomers' perceptions, is evidence of and reason for their lack of sophistication and prestige within the ballroom arena. Furthermore, the resources ballroom required helped the Regent's rural elites distinguish themselves as cosmopolitans. Through performance, ballroom dancers employed the symbolic dimensions of cultural capital to lay claim to a higher social position than they might otherwise assume they could hold. That position was occasionally explicitly named, but more often it was coded as a more "classy, beautiful performance."

This chapter served to introduce the wealth of symbolic resources the "ballroom umbrella" encompasses and the degree to which such expressive culture can be employed in performance for social projects. The remainder of this book is dedicated to a greater understanding of this process: the ways in which amateur hobbyist dancers perform their social reality and imaginatively forge new ones in dance and music.

2

Rules of Engagement

MARKETING SAFETY AND MANAGING RISK IN THE BALLROOM

Driving south out of Champaign, Illinois, one might completely fail to notice the low-lying residential landscape of the neighboring village of Savoy. From Savoy's small commercial district on Route 45—which includes a veterinary clinic, a Honda dealership, a Dairy Queen, a multiplex, and a Schnuck's grocery store—the 1970s residential neighborhoods that begin one block west are barely perceptible. Even less remarkable is the single-story, brick rectangle that lies between the dentist's office and a new funeral home: the Regent Ballroom and Banquet Center. With the building's cryptic storefront sign that announces simply "Regent" and its covered windows, only the packed parking lot on Friday night suggests that this is home to a vibrant social scene. In this way, ballroom is both nowhere and everywhere. Ballroom dance serves as an icon of heteronormative romance and desire, and, as such, it makes a regular appearance in Hollywood romances and advertisements for prescription drugs developed to treat sexual dysfunction.[1] Most Americans have heard at least a few popular ballroom dance songs and likely have even seen it performed in films or on television, at a wedding, or on a cruise. Many know someone who knows someone who has taken ballroom dance classes. However, the local sites of ballroom performance are often visible only to the select few who dance on a regular basis. The buildings are often nondescript, remote from commercial districts, and betray little of the energy they contain. Ballroom is simultaneously familiar and obscure, contemporary and outdated, popular and out of favor, mainstream and marginal. And so, those who entered the Regent did not stumble upon it by accident, they conducted some research and sought it out.

This chapter follows the trajectory of individuals as they enter the ballroom for the very first time and progress to become fluent ballroom dancers. It begins with a discussion of local practices at the Regent ballroom in Savoy, Illinois, and then examines how members of this particular local context connect with the more global aspects of ballroom performance.[2] I argue that a sense of safety, one of the primary commodities marketed in the ballroom, functions both to generate participation and maintain local communities as well as to provide the necessary components codified to ensure performance on an international scale.[3] Furthermore, feeling safe to dance without risk of physical harm or social rejection is a first requirement in realizing ballroom's promise of becoming beautiful.

Stepping in the Ballroom: Dancing in Savoy

Like virtually any American ballroom studio, the Regent is a commercial endeavor, and perhaps the most important and profitable commodity sold here—more so than the dance events, the instruction, the shoes, and so on—is safety. That is, the ballroom is a place where individuals can take risks of a personal, physical, and social nature, with a virtual safety net to prevent them from losing too much in the process. Safety is one of the most pervasive reasons people choose ballroom dance over other kinds of social activities. Mark stated it most clearly:

> There are certain things about being here, those items, the fun parts, the social aspect of it is a big deal. I've always been a very asocial person. I didn't really care if people liked me or not. I would go to a party and sit in a chair and I would just watch people. If I get involved in conversations, that's fine, but if not, I'm ok with that too. But, I've always been really uncomfortable with it. [Ballroom] actually gave me rules for engagement, and certain ways to do things and you knew it was always safe, and certain things you could say when you say hello to somebody. It makes it so much easier with all these rules.

The "rules for engagement" are not only behavioral conventions governing the socializing between dances, as Mark suggests, but also conventions governing the movement itself. In fact, just about every aspect of ballroom dancing has an accompanying code of conduct that is made clear to participants in a variety of ways. The extensive catechism ensures that the buy-in for these rules of engagement is consistently high across the venue's clientele. This consistency and predictability of behavior—both in social interaction and physical deportment—ensure not only the physical safety of dancers but also their emotional well-being and social status. Problematic contexts that would leave them feeling socially, emotionally, or physically vulnerable are reduced to the point of elimination. The structure and conventions of ballroom dance offer the thrill of exposure—of opening oneself up to other people as well as the unfamiliar act of dancing in public—without the fear of rejection, judgment, or failure that often accompany these acts in other contexts.

Stepping In: First Classes

David Lin is a consummate businessman, and he considers himself distinct from many other ballroom dance studio owners because he understands that ballroom's marketability is rooted in the careful measure of personal risk within the provision of safety on various levels.[4] Attracting new clients is one of the most difficult aspects of the business, because before someone will give ballroom dancing a try, he or she must believe that it is not only fun and exciting but also possible and safe. To decide to try dancing as an adult, after a lifetime of believing oneself incapable of doing so (as is the case for most American ballroomers), is a bold move that strikes fear into the hearts of many. First-time dancers—even those who were excited about the possibility of learning to dance, but especially those who were dragged into it by a friend, spouse, or lover—literally tremble with fear in the arms of their partners. Regent advertisements let potential clients know that they would be safe, that they would have fun, and that success was possible. Advertisements also welcomed singles, letting them know that they need not have a partner to enroll in a class.

This was a lot of information to include in a small newspaper announcement or brief television commercial, and for this reason the best advertisement has proved to be word of mouth. Individuals who enjoy dancing often encourage friends to give it a try. Knowing there would be a friendly face at the class is sometimes enough incentive to get newcomers to their first class. David also offered a financial incentive: new customers could try the first four weeks of a twelve-week beginner class with no obligation to continue. This abbreviated commitment enticed people who were tempted but otherwise might not have given ballroom dance a try. For instance, Brett, a brawny, handsome, middle-aged widower and successful construction contractor, has been dancing for more than five years. But he states that the initial hurdle to believing himself capable of dancing was significant.

> JOANNA BOSSE: One of the things that I found interesting was that most people who dance ballroom didn't grow up dancing ballroom. Didn't grow up necessarily thinking of themselves as dancers, so for many dancers there's a real hurdle, . . .
>
> BRETT [interrupting]: Yes, it's huge. . . . Mine was huge. In fact when I first signed up, I only signed up for four weeks. If you sign up for the whole class you get a discount, and I'm terribly cheap and I would love the discount, but I knew I wouldn't last four weeks. There's no way I could possibly do this for more than four weeks. I probably wouldn't make it the four weeks. [pause] I had some issues that, I'm kinda shy, and being that close to a stranger I knew that would never work. . . . But I liked it.
>
> JB: Why did you sign up for it then?
>
> B: I wanted to do it, I always wanted to do that. I had read sometime that the best things you can do are the things you don't want to do. Public speaking, dancing, things like that, learn how to do those, and that's probably what made me come.
>
> JB: Because you were shy . . .
>
> B: Yeah. I was at a point in my life, my wife had died the year before and I had time and wanted to try something different.

This four-week incentive was packaged as a newspaper coupon that ran frequently, especially around the December holidays, near Valentine's Day, and just before the summer wedding season. It was also presented in the form of Christmas cards that are left out in a basket in the Regent lobby for regular customers to take and pass on as gifts. Thus personal endorsement and a popular financial incentive frequently work together. Mark's experience is common:

> Our neighbors from across the street from where we were living mentioned to us that they dance out here. [My wife, Jane] was interested. To me it was like, "Ballroom dance? What? Am I on the same planet? Why would I do this?" To me it was a completely foreign idea. And then, what happened was, she had another baby and the subject went away completely. And then when our youngest was three the subject came up again. I think it was one of those "she twisted my arm" and she twisted, and she looked for ways to twist it. "I have this coupon" [she said], "so we could get a few lessons really cheap." So I said, "Let's do this while it's really cheap and I can get you off my back about this." [He laughs.] I'm laughing, now, but I'm being serious about this.

The couple eventually went on to introduce several of their friends to ballroom. In fact, this interview took place in the lobby of the Regent while Mark was waiting for some of his friends who were attending a beginning ballroom class.

Some of the most basic rules of engagement of ballroom are made explicit to newcomers. The Regent, like many ballroom dance organizations and clubs across the country, publishes a "New Student Information" form. In fact, a cursory search on the Internet will lead to numerous such fact pages posted by college and community dance organizations as well as by professional studios. The Regent's information page, distributed to students in Ballroom I (the class for people with no prior dance instruction), strives to put newcomers at ease by using enthusiastic and welcoming language to introduce some of the basic social conventions. The information included on this sheet as well as that provided by the instructor in the first classes makes clear the personal obligations of each dancer. For example, students are told, "Because social ballroom dance requires close partner contact, please be aware of proper personal hygiene. For your convenience, mints can be purchased at the front desk." The variables of social convention are explicitly articulated to ensure consistent adherence to these standards on the part of all dancers. It also helps beginners know what to wear, how to behave, and what to expect of others.

Extending beyond issues of hygiene, however, is a concern for appearance: "Dress for class should be comfortable and lend to free movement. We suggest avoiding shorts, blue jeans, t-shirts, etc. . . . Proper footwear is important. A lightweight, securely fit leathered sole shoe is most appropriate." Many dancers like the fact that ballroom is "classy," and one way the higher-class status of the genre is communicated is through the dress code. As a poor graduate student conducting research on this topic, I was initially unable to afford new clothes and attended the early classes dressed in faded blue jeans and cowboy boots (the only leather-soled shoes I owned). I was not turned away (though explicit, the social conventions of dance are not compulsory), but I felt conspicuous as one of the few to wear casual denim and was occasionally subjected to good-natured but pointed teasing about my wardrobe from fellow dancers.

The dress code is also important because dress is one common way social groups communicate affinity and difference. With the exception of one couple in their twenties, no one at the Regent wore tattoos, piercings, torn or shredded clothes, or any other external markers of "alternative" or urban lifestyles that would suggest any type of social edge or irony within this earnest crowd. The Regent's clientele was largely middle-and upper-middle-class white midwesterners, and the dress code resembled what many of these individuals wore in other social situations. Men typically wore dress slacks in neutral muted colors of khaki, tan, black, blue, or gray with a colored, casual-dress, collared shirt, and leather dress shoes. Women enjoyed a greater variety of wardrobe, alternating between dress slacks and skirts or dresses. They wore leather dress shoes with heels or dance shoes purchased from the Regent or on the Internet. The apparent contradiction between a dress code that encouraged clothes that are "comfortable and lend to free movement" and a reality that discouraged clothes designed for comfort and physical activity (t-shirts, shorts, athletic shoes, workout wear) is explained only when taking into consideration the primary role of wardrobe in affirming a shared, middle-class identity. Although no one stated it in such terms, I also suspect that the dress clothes were important in the genre's ability to make one feel beautiful within this class-based context. A skirt flowing fluidly around one's calves is a sensorial experience of movement that workout wear does not provide.[5]

The homogeneity of dress style ensured by social pressure and the explicit dress code allows newcomers to immediately feel that they were among friends—or at least among people like themselves. Upon entering the ballroom for their first class, dancers feel at ease as they look around the room and see people who look very much like themselves: predominantly white, heterosexual, middle-class suburbanites in skirts and blouses, khakis and button-downs.

The explicit rules of engagement also discussed social obligations to fellow dancers. The Regent form states: "We would like everyone to become acquainted with each other. Therefore, we require everyone to wear a name tag, which we will provide." During class, teachers direct students to greet their new partners, introduce themselves, and always say "thank you" before leaving the partnership. David's request was routine, and dancers heard it at least twenty times in one class: "Thank this partner and move on to the next, please." This behavior became so routinized that it was soon easy for even the shyest individuals to participate in these basic social conventions. Mark suggests that engaging in this basic ritual with every person in the room as dancers rotated partners helped him feel at ease and made it possible for him to develop new social skills:

> M: So for me, it was really beneficial in terms of just being able to be with other people in the sense that you have to greet them and say hello to them and do something I could never do before, which was make small talk. Before it was like, "I have no idea what to say."
>
> JB: I've noticed that in the classes, as you rotate partners, you comment on what you just learned or what you're about to do or [say] "Hi, how are you?" and just when you're about out of material, Dave starts talking about the next move and you don't have to . . .

M: Right. Or you're talking about something completely different. Ha! So if the class seems to be going slow, you walk up and say, "So, how did that go last week?" or whatever. So that was unexpected and what made it fun for me. It was not only entertaining, [it was] sort of a social learning experience for me as well as a learning dance. And not just, . . . it's something that has carried over to other types of activities and stuff. So now when I go to a party today, I'm still comfortable sitting in a chair watching what people are doing, but I'm also as comfortable standing and talking with people and asking them about things and stuff like that.

JB: Using those skills that you learned in ballroom?

M: Yes. So it was a skill set. You get more than learning dancing skills, [because] you can't avoid it. You're dancing with lots of other people, you have to learn how to be—I don't want to say not obnoxious—but you want to be friendly, you want people to have a good time with you.

Mastering the basic "rules for engagement" has proved to be transformational for many dancers, as we hear in Mark's testimony. His understanding of who he is as an embodied social being has been changed because of the new habits he has put in place through dance. Ritualizing these basic forms of casual social interaction helped increase the comfort level of many individuals, like Mark and Brett, who may have felt awkward or ill at ease touching and interacting with strangers.

One of the things rarely commented upon by dancers, but an aspect I believe central to experience in these early days of instruction, is the normalizing of touch and physical contact. Dancing causes anxiety in nondancers for many reasons, and one of them is the physical intimacy and contact the genre requires. It was an utterly common experience to feel the hands of my partner tremble in my own as we took our initial steps together. Over the weeks of lessons and dancing with dozens of partners (most of them strangers), individuals became familiar with the intimate act of just being in another's frame, in their space. That physical intimacy loses some of the kinetic and emotional charge as it becomes part of a dancer's habit, and one of the indicators of a dancer's skill was the ease with which he or she takes a partner in his or her arms, the confidence with which the dancer holds another's hand, and the complete lack of self-consciousness or embarrassment that such an act often produces in novices. With its intimate physical embrace, the subtlety of communicative signs, and the synchronic movement with a wide number of partners, social partnership dancing requires a great deal of trust. Generating a warm and welcoming social space is a crucial first step toward creating an environment conducive to such widespread trust and feelings of security.

Stepping It Up: Intermediate Classes

Early in my work I ran into Martin, a single, white male in his early thirties, as he was leaving his first ever dance class. I knew him from another context and was surprised to see him dancing. His face was flushed and he was very animated. I asked him, "Well, what do you think? Did you like it?" He replied, "Are you kidding me? Like it? I loved it! What's not to love? In about an hour, I touched, like, thirty women! I didn't have to worry about any of them rejecting me, and by the end of the class we were actually dancing! It may not have been great, but we were doing it together, it was amazing!"

If the marketing of success in a socially safe environment is paramount to ballroom's ability to attract newcomers, keeping them depends on the genre's ability to deliver on that promise. Here the nature of ballroom dance pedagogy, standardized and codified over the last one hundred years, helps to create the safe climate necessary for individuals to overcome their anxieties about public dancing. David, for instance, unites a number of complementary pedagogical strategies with a singular philosophy about amateur dancing: "It has to be fun first. For you it's different [referencing the fact that I teach at a university], fun doesn't matter. But for me, if it isn't fun, I'm out of business. They'll just quit."

In the beginning classes, teachers at the Regent eliminated choices, determining for students everything related to the structural components of the dance: in what direction they faced, in what direction they moved, what steps they performed, when to begin and stop moving, when to change partners, and the like. Although this may seem restrictive, in fact the students found it liberating. They make choices all day for work or family, and they enjoy being released from leadership duties to enjoy themselves, their partners, and the pleasure of moving their bodies to music.

In Regent classes, the dancers did not exercise personal choice even in their selection of partners. They exchanged partners in rotation as determined by the teacher and danced with each partner they encountered in their path.[6] Over the course of a single class meeting, they danced with every class member of the opposite sex, regardless of how they felt about each one individually—hence Martin's comment about dancing without fear of rejection. Dancers of the opposite sex were required to dance with him regardless of how they felt about it. Some couples occasionally complained about this mandate early on in their instruction, and they either quit or came to understand the benefits of such a strategy to their dancing and enjoyed the camaraderie that resulted from dancing with their class cohort.

Unlike competitive dancers, who generally study and perform with one partner, social dancers often learn to dance with many partners. In fact, all of the studios I studied required partner exchange in order to prevent partners from anticipating the moves of their home partner and accommodating for one another's mistakes. The benefits of exchanging partners becomes self-evident quickly in the early classes, and soon even those who are most nervous about changing partners eventually become happy to do so.[7]

The importance of changing partners in class is also linked to convention within social dance contexts. Ballroom dance stands somewhat apart from other kinds of American social partnership dancing in that it is entirely appropriate, common, and encouraged to ask a perfect stranger to dance. Social conventions within the other kinds of American partnership dances generally restrict such behavior, with occasional exceptions for pursuing romantic interests. Small groups and social cliques form the basic social unit at many commercial venues for salsa and country dancing, for instance, and it is not uncommon for individuals who transgress such boundaries to receive rejections to their invitations. Ballroom dancers are far less likely to directly reject an invitation to dance, even if from a stranger, although it is sometimes the case that they will avoid or postpone an invitation, taking a rain check for later in the evening. This is one reason for the attention given to creating a safe space: because the convention deems it inappropriate to turn down an invitation, it is incumbent upon the community to create a trustworthy and safe environment.[8] This building of community takes place beginning with one's initial entrance into the ballroom and is facilitated and strengthened by the insistence on switching partners right from the first lesson.

The elimination of personal choice at the outset extends from partner selection to the actual dance performance. Like other creative arts, dance is somewhat intimidating for those who have never tried it, in part because of the perception that it relies on talent and individual inspiration. Artistic freedom can be scary, especially for those who do not believe themselves to be artistically talented. Wrenching dance from prevailing notions of talent, ballroom classes are highly structured and regimented and begin with such rudimentary steps that even the most inexperienced students keep up. At the early stages, individuals are essentially walking around the room. Walking, a skill that all participants have mastered, incrementally becomes dancing, and nondancers metamorphose into dancers.

Although not stated as such, the Regent employed a "no student left behind" policy when it came to dance instruction. Classes moved very slowly and began with a review of what was introduced in the last class. Some couples practiced throughout the week, but most did not. Thus, the classes introduced material quite slowly and involved much repetition from one week to the next. Although some of the younger, college-age students complained about this pace, very few of the other students did, and those who wanted a faster pace of instruction were often encouraged to skip ahead to the next class, perhaps with a private lesson or two to prepare them for the more difficult material. For newcomers who did not practice between classes, however, the standard pace was challenging but not overwhelming.

The lessons were built on a few basic pedagogical principles, all of which relied on extensive verbal description and explanation as well as demonstrations. One involved the reduction of movement into the smallest units, or cells, isolated by body parts. Students first learned to move their feet in rhythm, after which they then learned the direction the steps should take. Arm movements were introduced next, followed by the mechanics of lead and follow—what foot and arm movements were critical for directing one's partner or accepting the lead properly. Only after the footwork and arm movements were ingrained (which may take several classes or even several levels of coursework) would the teacher move on to the less obvious components of the step—for instance, the direction of the head and face; how the hip, knee, or ankle contribute to the style of the footwork; or the subtle use of the torso for improving connection as well as line and style. The isolation of body parts allowed students to focus on one part of their body at any given moment. As the components were introduced and layered one over the other—first the feet, then the arms, then the head and the knee, and eventually the torso—the complete dance step began to emerge. This level of competency, however, is achieved only through several levels of class instruction.

Typical dance steps, and especially the simplest ones, take place over as few as four measures of music. To be able to dance to a complete song, students must string together sequences of dance steps. Once several steps were learned through the isolation technique described in the paragraph above, students learned the strategies and transitional steps necessary to segue from one move to another. This kind of compartmentalized, rationalized dance instruction is not the manner in which couple dance needs be learned (see, for example, Berrios-Miranda 2003), but it does resonate with the sensibilities of this group of elites who were trained in American educational systems and universities, where isolating variables is standard practice.

In fact, David cultivates as much resemblance as possible between his dance classes and American university classes. The Regent curriculum was ordered around a regular, annual schedule of offerings called "semesters." The dance partners who assist the teachers were called "teaching assistants," were considered subservient to the teacher, and were discouraged from speaking directly to the students during the lessons with some exceptions. Furthermore, as mentioned in the previous chapter, David often incorporated scientific principles and metaphors into his classes as a means for clarifying certain points. Sometimes he named these laws of physics explicitly, and other times he used metaphor to communicate the core ideas without relying on scientific vocabulary. Whether using the laws of physics or examples from everyday life, this pedagogical approach appealed to his students' sensibilities in terms of the way they understood movement—as driven by a set of physical laws and principles and chains of cause and effect. It also earned David credibility among his clientele, who respect him in part for being a good teacher and a well-educated man.

Through descriptions based on the laws of motion and physics, students learned that dance is simply about motion and countermotion, rather than a language of emotion or artistry. They were tacitly discouraged from thinking of their performance as resulting from the more mysterious and laden concepts of artistry and talent. The formulaic nature of sequencing steps together and routinizing certain combinations is where creativity was located, and its nature, as explained in ballroom, was demystified. Dancing, elementary ballroom classes teach us, is not about a blank canvas on which to perform our self-expression; it is instead the mastery of a vocabulary of pre-choreographed steps sequenced together in logical order.

Furthermore, David emphasizes to his beginning students that the difference between them and the more advanced dancers at the Friday night dances is simply one of "mileage." "Many of them started right where you are, but they were worse!" he often jokes, cultivating the low-pressure, good-humored, noncompetitive learning environment on which he has staked his reputation.

The tenor of the classroom is one of the most important qualities to ensuring student success. Eschewing an emphasis on judgment and competition, Regent teachers constantly draw on empathy, humor, and constant encouragement during class. Retelling stories from their own days as beginners, they relate with empathy the frustration of learning a difficult move and even demonstrated their own literal missteps in comic self-deprecation. Downplaying (if not completely removing) the concepts of talent, judgment, and competition from the learning of dance allows students to feel more comfortable in class and to believe that they are capable of dancing well, even during the most difficult lessons. Moving their bodies according to certain laws and rules, nondancers slowly begin to see a performance, a dance, emerge. They witness the transformation and credit the dance itself as its source.

Given the highly standardized nature of the dance and the pedagogy, one might assume that students would find the classes staid. For the most part, this was far from the truth.[9] First, the novelty of moving to music in and of itself was such a departure from the everyday that many find that aspect alone is enough to keep them engaged. This is especially so for older students or those in less-than-ideal health, for whom such movement is physically demanding.

Second, although the pace of the courses is quite slow in terms of the introduction of new material, the pace of any given class session feels faster because of the rapid partner exchange and frequent repetition. A lesson may focus on a simple, four-beat pattern, for example, but the move is then practiced a number of times with several partners in rapid succession, allowing dancers to feel how the step is reinvented anew within each partnership. Although the teachers use a great deal of language, they are careful to avoid talking for too long (no more than five minutes) before having the students perform. For most dancers, the pace of the classes seemed quick and engaging even though the introduction of actual new material is relatively slow and deliberate.[10]

Finally, the social aspect of the classroom dynamic also keeps students engaged. Each partner exchange permits brief moments of socialization during the breaks from the class narrative that allowed students to relax, socialize with someone new, and then regroup for one more attempt. This rapid-fire sequence of one-on-one social encounters is particularly refreshing. The kinesthetic experience of touching another person while moving to music is, in many ways, its own reward that begets more energy. As the students pair up anew to take one more pass at the move, the classroom environment feels more like a game than a lesson. "What do you think, can we do this?" a new partner asked me as he approached for one more attempt at the "twin cities" pattern during the swing lesson. "I don't know," I replied. "Let's give it a try and see where we end up." A spirit of collaboration was born not only through the actual performance of the genre but through the nature of the pedagogy itself, which eliminated rejection as a possibility and replaced it with esprit de corps.

Stepping Out on the Town: "Doing It in the Dark"

After having been away for three years, I returned to the Regent for a Tuesday night "practice dance." Between songs David welcomed me back with a hug and celebrated my homecoming with an announcement over the PA system. This prompted familiar faces and new ones to make their way over to me eventually and to greet the woman "writing a book on ballroom." Among the new faces was Arnold, a married, middle-aged dancer who was interested to hear about my project. After we talked a while and I learned that he had been dancing for three years, I asked him if he would join me for a foxtrot, one of his favorite dances. "Oh, no, I couldn't." he said nervously, "I don't know enough moves for you. Maybe the next rumba instead?" I was sorry to have put him on the spot, and was surprised to find that even during the rumba he trembled as we danced, searching his memory for moves like an ill-prepared sophomore searches desperately for answers during a geometry exam.

While beginner dancers hid in the comfort of classes for the first weeks and even years of their instruction, inevitably they ventured out for an evening of social dancing. Performing a move in class is one thing, but dancers say you cannot really know if you have it until you can "do it in the dark"—that is, until you perform it in real time under the low lights of a club or formal dance setting. The Regent provided two opportunities for such dancing: the Tuesday night practice dances and the more formal Friday night dances.

The Regent's Tuesday night practice dances were generally the first stop until David ceased hosting them in favor of offering more classes. They were called "practice dances" because they merged the ambience of an evening of social dance (the low lighting, a Deejay playing complete songs, and other dancers all moving freely around the floor) with the nurturing environment of a class (teachers nearby to help in a jam, the freedom to stop and start in the middle of a song if things go awry, and low expectations among all the dancers in attendance). For these events the bar was open only during the break to serve soft drinks, there was no printed dance card, the dress code was more casual than the more formal events, and the chairs were aligned along the perimeter of the wall rather than around tables with candlelight (as is customary for Friday night events). In essence, Tuesday nights functioned as simulations of actual dance events such as the more formal Friday night dances, described in detail during the interludes herewith.

In class, students learned short steps and to sequence these steps eventually into longer moves that could take a few seconds to perform. Dancing to an entire three- to four-minute song caused some anxiety, especially for men like Arnold, because beginners know only enough moves for about a minute of dancing. Until they add more moves to their repertoire, dancers must repeat material while working to make their performance seem more varied than it really is. Such techniques involved changing directions, employing subtle variations of arm movement, inserting basic steps in different places, and so forth. Women desired the ability to respond to these moves smoothly, as if they have danced them before even when they have not. In this context of live dancing, as opposed to classroom work, the obligation to please one's partner becomes more real and the pressure is greater—thus Arnold's concern that he may not be "good enough" to provide an enjoyable dance experience for me.

Pleasing one's partner in a dance is one component of a larger obligation to "take care" of one's partner and fellow dancers—that is, keeping them safe from harm as the dancers move through space. Regent dancers used this term often when discussing their obligations to one another, highlighting the importance of safety in both the physical and social sense. Although it was most often framed as one of the male leader's responsibilities to "take care of his partner," this obligation extended to followers as well and, to a certain degree, to couples as they moved about one another on the dance floor.

"Taking care" begins with the most basic social etiquette and thanking one's partner after a dance. For older male dancers who learned to dance in an earlier era, it may also entail escorting a partner from her seat to the floor and back again after the dance is over. But the obligation extends beyond these simple social rules to the dance itself. It involves not stepping on a partner's feet, maintaining one's own balance and not pulling a partner off-balance, as well as not using excessive or abrupt force that may cause partners to experience pain in their fingers, wrists, elbows, shoulders, or knees. The forward-moving member of the couple (who is most often the leader) is also responsible for making sure the backward moving partner does not run into or step on anyone else.[11]

For men, the obligation to "take care of one's partner" also means assessing his partner's skill level and leading her in moves that match her abilities. Howard, for instance, was notorious as someone who did not "take care" of his partners in this way. Criticized for showing off his own skills rather than attending to the needs of his partner, he often led women in moves that were beyond their capabilities. Interestingly, many women loved this tightrope-style performance. When they finished a dance without incident, they left the floor, their faces flushed with excitement and smiling an exhausted and relieved smile.[12] Just as frequently, however, Howard's partner would have to stop in the middle of the dance to regroup because she missed a lead or did not know the step, causing feelings of embarrassment. On such occasions, onlookers explicitly expressed their disdain for this aspect of Howard's style, suggesting that he was selfish, acting inappropriately and placing his partners in compromising positions.

William, however, was a favorite partner among women, because he took very seriously his role of "taking care" not to lead his partner in moves that would be uncomfortable either physically or socially. He was adept at assessing a partner's abilities and matching his leads to her skill level so that she was not self-conscious about the limits of her ability or worried that she was preventing William from having a good time. Another dancer, however, criticized William for not "taking care" of the other couples. As a highly skilled dancer, William was capable of dancing at high speeds with rapid changes of direction. When dancing with an equally skilled partner, William would weave in and between the slower-moving couples on the floor, sometimes disorienting them by moving out of pace and with changes in direction the lesser dancers could not anticipate. Although he tried to be careful, he occasionally bumped into or stepped on the toes of lesser dancers. While technically the fault may have been considered to lie with the lesser dancers, who are notorious for not keeping their feet squarely under their own bodies, advanced dancers attributed the blame to William and his partner for not "taking care" of the other couples on the floor. Thus, dancers are obligated to one another for both the social comfort as well as the physical safety of their partner and that of others on the dance floor.

Alcohol and "Taking Care"

The emphasis on safety and "taking care" extends to other aspects of performance, such as limiting the consumption of alcohol and drugs during a dance.[13] Sobriety is considered a key requirement not only for the technical demands of the genre but also for the social and physical demands of "taking care" of your partner and keeping the dance floor safe. Excessive consumption was not only taboo at the Regent, it was made explicit on the information form for new students, which states, "As a courtesy to fellow dancers, we ask that you please do not have any alcoholic drinks before class."

The convention of sobriety carried over into social dance events as well. Although the Regent opens its full bar for Friday night dances, alcohol sales are quite low. In my experience tending bar for these events, which often hosted more than two hundred dancers, I rarely sold more than five glasses of wine and one or two mixed drinks the entire evening. The Regent offers a free bottle of champagne (or sparkling grape juice) to those celebrating a birthday or anniversary, but even this was customarily shared among a large number of friends and fellow dancers, ensuring that no one person drank an inappropriate amount. I never witnessed a ballroom dancer drink excessively at a dance, and I never perceived anyone in attendance as having compromised faculties due to the consumption of any substance. Once during my time at the Regent, however, David was asked to speak to a novice student who arrived having had consumed alcohol and whose performance was considered sloppy by his fellow students. The conventions of the genre have resulted in a context in which this kind of self-policing is the norm.[14]

Relative to other kinds of social dancing at local clubs and bars, where alcohol is considered a prerequisite for "loosening up" before entering the dance floor, ballroom dancers are distinct for their sobriety, which they deem necessary to fulfill their obligation to "take care" of their partners as well as other dancing couples. This kind of attention to physical safety is especially important to dancers and depends on a sober awareness of one's surroundings. The reputation of the Regent as a safe space was built, in part, upon this sobriety. Perhaps better stated, one of the primary aversions ballroom dancers have to dancing at local clubs and bars in this college town is the pervasive influence of liquor they find at such establishments. Drunkenness and the accompanying loss of motor control causes dancers to bump into one another, sometimes with glass beer bottles or cigarettes in hand. Furthermore, dance floors made sticky with spilt liquor impede dancers' abilities to glide smoothly across the floor. For these reasons, ballroom dancers find excessive liquor a problematic influence that compromises the quality of the dance experience, making it unlikely that they would lose themselves in the dance moment. For example, Louise, a thirty-something professional, prefers to ballroom dance, explaining, "I'm very sensitive to cigarette smoke, and there's generally no smoking there [in the ballroom], and no freaky people getting drunk. Dancers will have a drink or two, and then they're dancing, and that's always who I was. I'm not into the smoking scene. I'm not into the bar-drinking-a-ton scene. So it's a social place to enjoy music, have a drink on a Friday night, and get away from work."

Drunkenness is also considered problematic because it is often accompanied by a loss of inhibitions that could lead to sexually charged situations and physical altercations. As one divorced ballroom dancer stated, "I want to go out, I want to meet people, I may even want a drink, but I don't want to go to a meat market. That's not for me. There aren't many options besides the Regent." Many dancers contrasted the safety of the Regent with the danger of "meat markets"; concern over the predatory nature of a number of dance clubs drove many dancers to the Regent, where overt communication of sexual attraction within a dance is generally inappropriate; in fact, it may be difficult for an outsider to the genre to determine which dancing couples are actually romantic partners as well. William provides an example from his performance with fellow dancer, Jill:

> In one of the university classes, one of the things that beginners have trouble with, singles especially, is the idea that when you're dancing with someone there's a different rule of what you're allowed to do with them than when you aren't dancing with them. So when the music stops it's like you revert back to normal. Take Jill, for example. I don't know if you interviewed her or not, but she's a perfect example of that because she's Mormon, extremely conservative. When you put her in a dance dress on the dance floor and the music goes on, you can flirt with

> her outrageously and she flirts back. And then the music goes off, and we're back to the old rules. And some people don't understand that. Beginners try to carry on the intimacy [when they] walk off the floor with the person. People ask me how I can dance with Jill like that when she is married. And I'm like, because it's dancing. You know, it's just letting down the rules, and having a good time, and knowing that when the music is off you haven't insulted her or anything [laughs].

This is unlike other kinds of American social dancing. For instance, in my experience performing salsa, merengue, bachata, country two-step, Argentine tango, and solo rock dancing, I found it not at all uncommon for romantic couples to signal their attraction on the dance floor to onlookers and to one another (perhaps for the first time). In these contexts, dancers employ a number of signals of varying subtlety to express romantic interest within a dance. They include placing hands on a partner's intimate body parts (such as low hips and buttocks), wrapping arms completely around a partner to ensure shoulder-to-knee contact, stroking a partner's hair or face, dancing literally cheek to cheek, looking directly into one another's eyes, and other idiosyncratic gestures. Occasionally, one member of the partnership does not welcome these signals, leading to awkward and perhaps stressful moments, and in rare instances even violence.

This kind of experience was virtually unheard of among Regent dancers, not because ballroom dancers do not experience romantic attraction for one another, but because it is generally inappropriate to overtly communicate such attraction within a dance. Such an expression violates the obligation to take care of one's partner, to keep him or her safe and comfortable. Ballroom dancers rely much more on the time between songs and socializing before or after dance events for opportunities to further potential romantic couplings. This is not to say that the genre is not sexualized; rather, such signs of sexual attraction are theatrical and are not meant to communicate genuine feelings of sexual attraction between two members of a dancing couple (Gainor 2007; McMains 2006).

The reputation of ballroom as a "safe" genre in this context was predicated on the comparison of the Regent to other kinds of local social dance contexts, which, as suggested above, were perceived as intimidating or predatorial, if not dangerous. By comparison, ballroom appears pure and edifying, perpetuating a discourse of ennoblement begun by ballroom dance masters at the turn of the twentieth century.

It is important to note that unlike participants in other social dance contexts, ballroom dancers typically begin with classes. With absolutely no instruction it is very difficult for newcomers to perform ballroom dance, and this awareness seems to have been intuited by most, for few individuals uninitiated in the genre attend Friday night dances. Rather, they typically call the Regent after having seen an ad in the paper or having heard about ballroom from a friend, and they enroll in the first weeks of the beginner class. Ballroom is thus unlike other social dance contexts in which people learn "on the fly" during a social event among dancers with a wide range of abilities, performing for an entire song by imitating others. For many who choose ballroom, this kind of initiation is itself a scary thing. The "sink or swim" model can be a source of discomfort, especially to older dancers, newly single individuals who experience anxiety about entering an unfamiliar social climate alone, and those who feel less adept at physical improvisation or with their social skills.

With the exception of university clubs, all other social couple dancing in the region occurred in the context of bars, where alcohol sales drove the marketing and management decisions (Bosse 2009). Bar owners encouraged deejays to compete for larger crowds and threatened to switch formats or deejays on a whim were they unable to turn the desired profit. In this rural area, cover charges were low (between two and three dollars, if they were employed at all), and the take at the door was the deejay's compensation, putting the onus on the deejay for advertising and turning out large crowds.

Such dance contexts were considered less safe by ballroom dancers for several reasons. First, the prevalence of alcohol and concern for high alcohol sales on the part of club owners created an environment radically different from that experienced in ballroom. Intoxication was not uncommon, and the presence of alcohol on the dance floor was the norm. Bouncers were often barely able to contain the potential for violence (though these usually took the form of petty fistfights between jealous romantic rivals). Furthermore, bartenders and managers were generally rude to ballroom dancers when they attended dance events in their establishments because ballroomers arrived early, monopolized several tables, and rarely drank more than water or an occasional soda.

A second and perhaps more important point of comparison is the fact that in this region, undergraduate university students dominated the social scene in most dance clubs. The majority of ballroomers were in their thirties or older, and they felt conspicuous among the large crowds of potentially intoxicated undergraduates; the youngest ballroom dancers felt decidedly unhip and old when surrounded by the exuberant youth. As one young graduate student dancer complained after the Regent began hosting late-night salsa events, "They [salsa dancers] walk in here, all cool and beautiful, and take over the place. This is my place and now it feels like high school all over again with the cool kids taking over everything."

A third reason ballroom dancers felt unsafe in nonballroom venues was that all of the other local dance clubs changed formats every night. Bradley's, for example, hosted country dancing on Wednesday, rhythm and blues dancing on Thursday, hip hop dancing on Friday, a live band on Saturday (and the genre or format of these live performances changed radically from week to week), and widely varying events on Sunday (country dancing, open mic night, or something entirely different). At whim this schedule was changed to accommodate traveling musical acts, deejays who were ill or out of town, and so forth. This lack of consistency was common practice in the smaller towns across the Midwest. Because no one constituency proved profitable for a dance club every night of the week, management worked to attract all of them throughout the week. This rapid change and unpredictability of formats was exacerbated by the frequent changing of ownership and formats. While attempting to attract the broadest range of audiences, this aspect of the small-town entertainment industry also caused patrons to feel unsure about who was hosting what kind of dancing at any one time (see Bosse 2013b, 2013c).

The Regent, by comparison, was predictable—a "sure thing" that hosted ballroom dancing every Friday night and had done so for decades. The unchanging nature of the Regent allowed dancers to feel safe to change themselves. This consistency is a central key to ballroom's commercial success and part and parcel of its worldwide popularity as well. Repetition has proved to be an important element in performance at micro and macro levels, serving to bring people in, induce altered states, and create a greater sense of community (Becker 2004; Rouget 1985; Turino 2008).

The highly codified nature of ballroom dance allows for very little variance in performance practice across venues, a fact that has been parodied in any number of films about the genre, most famously in the cult favorite *Strictly Ballroom* (Bosse 2007). But such strict guidelines also ensure an unusually high degree of uniformity in performance literally across the globe. And so while dancers occasionally expressed frustration with the Regent's lack of spontaneity, they reveled in the benefits such rigid adherence to standardized practice affords—namely, that they could enjoy dancing with a complete stranger in a foreign locale. For example, Matthew, a computer programmer who traveled domestically and internationally for both work and pleasure, spoke with great enthusiasm about dancing in new clubs on his trips.

> M: I've had dances, like with a person I've never seen before. I don't know her name, and we'll have the most fantastic dance. There's something interesting in that, isn't there? Especially because we haven't taken from the same teacher, and . . .
>
> JB: You probably didn't even learn to dance in the same state.
>
> M: Right. I'm doing steps she probably doesn't even know. Now that's cool. There's something really cool about that. . . . The best is when it is with complete strangers.

Louise, who traveled frequently for work, pleasure, and dance opportunities, found it gratifying to travel to swing clubs around the country and see familiar faces from previous trips. She explained, "You can go to any city and find someone [to dance with]. You can at least watch even if you're not going to blend in. But now I've been to enough things that I can go to a West Coast dance and see three or four people I have danced with before. Even if I don't know their names, we recognize each other. It makes my world a little bigger than the small town I grew up in."

Ballroom is a global phenomenon (at least in metropolitan centers), and being able to travel to foreign places and find that you can connect with complete strangers through dance is, in and of itself, a rewarding experience. In addition, it affirms the merit of the genre as currency within cosmopolitan circles as well as a belief in its universality.[15]

One of the most striking aspects of ballroom dance is its symbolic significance internationally—its efficacy as a locally specific phenomenon and nexus for an international, intercontinental affinity group. As a preeminent expressive form during late colonization and the High Modern period, ballroom dance is embedded in cosmopolitan formations and performed in urban centers around the world. Ballroom arises among particular social groups in dispersed locales and has become what ethnomusicologist Thomas Turino called a "specific type of cultural formation and constitution of habitus that is translocal in purview" (2000, 7).[16]

Ballroom dance is not specific to a single or even a few neighboring locales. Rather, it is situated in many sites that are connected not by geographical proximity but by other forms of contact, media, and interchanges, including international competitions (annual, short-term events); print, visual, and audio media; and internet sites and discussion lists. Most important—and this is especially true of ballroom dancers—"cosmopolitan groups are connected across space by a similar constitution of habitus itself, which creates the foundation for social communication, alliances, and competition" (Turino 2000, 8). Although this book is, in essence, a foray into the shared aspects of habitus for a local group of midwestern social ballroom dancers, the cosmopolitan nature of ballroom dancing results in commonalities across regional and nation-state boundaries (Anderson 1981). This shared habitus allows ballroom dancers to travel the world and find complete strangers with whom to enjoy a complicated, circumscribed, and yet spontaneous dance experience. And so, although ballroom is not a signifier of a common cultural, ethnic, or even singular class status, the aspects of habitus shared by the members of this affinity group ensure acceptance of the particular kind of regulation and codification for which ballroom is both celebrated and maligned. This standardization subsequently ensures consistency of performance practice around the world and the ability to travel throughout the world performing the genre successfully.

The affective potential of this experience is not to be underestimated. Ballroom dance, when performed with anyone, is an expression of a basic human need—to know we are not alone, to know someone is listening, and to feel another respond to us. But when this experience is enjoyed with a complete stranger—and the more foreign the partner the more powerful the lesson—it takes one beyond feeling "in community" with some*one* to a confirmation of the unlimited potential for community in humanity. In this sense, ballroom's highly codified and structured nature is a requisite component of such an experience. However, as the Australian film *Strictly Ballroom* lampoons the genre specifically for its perceived rigidity, scholars, too, have derided this aspect of many upper-class genres of European derivation precisely because it is believed to impede spontaneous, creative play and communitas. One might argue that impeding collective participation is precisely the point of some European-derived arts, but it is also important to remember that music and dance contexts capable of generating feelings of connectedness are not the purview of any particular socioeconomic class, race, or geographic region.[17] Although particular structural components exist that may be more and less likely to generate a participatory ethos (see Feld 1984, 1988; Keil and Feld 1994; Keil 1987, 1995; Turino 2008), what determines their affective potential is the degree to which safety and risk are managed relative to the general disposition (habitus) of its participants. One person's "uptight" is another's "just right" when it comes to joining in and feeling connected. The structural elements of the genre, the performance context, the pedagogical model, and the movement itself—all cultural manifestations of a shared habitus—establish the parameters of safety and are generative of the feeling of being safe.

Social ballroom dance, then, provides an opportunity for individuals to be creative—to engage movement and music—in a public and social space without risk of rejection or failure. Through its places and pedagogies, the genre provides the context and tools necessary for nondancers to become dancers—to become creative, artistic individuals capable of creating something beautiful in cooperation with others. American social ballroom dance presents an array of commodities for consumption, but I suggest that it is this opportunity for transformation that accounts for its continued presence in American social life.

Interlude

A quiet rumba gives way to the cheerful refrain of a quickstep, and I see Dean making his way toward me for the dance I promised him earlier in the evening. Dean is a single, white, thirty-something astrophysicist—literally, a rocket scientist—and a wonderful smooth dancer. After a brief moment to set up, we're off for what seems like the sprint of ballroom dance. The fast pace of the dance causes beginners to panic a bit, and they rush the steps. For this reason, David schedules two in a set with the intention that couples will take turns, either dancing the first or second, leaving the floor a little more open and easier to navigate. In practice, it does not work out this way. Everyone simply dances two quicksteps with two different partners, and I will take my place on the floor with Leo for the second.

The optimistic quality of quickstep songs—in this case, an instrumental version of "Lazy, Hazy, Crazy Days of Summer"—is matched sonically by the floating quality of the dance. As Dean and I turn the far corner of the floor, our feet, it seems, move rapidly, specifically, while our upper bodies—fixed in closed position—feel light, ethereal, betraying (at least in my imagination) not a trace of the busy footwork happening below. I break into a private grin, imagining that I might look something like Wile E. Coyote after just running beyond the edge of the cliff, my legs a frenzied blur under a perfectly quiet upper body. I slowly move my head from left to right and then left again as we turn the corner. This gesture always makes me feel like a more accomplished dancer than I am. Although my quickstep is not that strong, Dean's is quite good, and I imagine the two of us—both young, tall and moving with assurance around the floor—strike a handsome figure. The most advanced dancers certainly recognize the many flaws with my quickstep, one of my weakest dances, but as we circle the floor, I notice a number of others watching in admiration and gesturing to their friends as we pass. Knowing this, I check my posture in the mirrors that line the long walls of the ballroom—lowering my shoulders (which rise habitually when I am challenged), engaging my core, elongating my neck and back—and attend more carefully to the placement of my feet.

Dean is one of my favorite partners for smooth dances, and I think they are the genres he performs best—amenable to his tall posture, high center of gravity, the calm that passes over his face when he dances, and the fact that he does not use his body to punctuate the musical accents. He was disappointed when I communicated this to him—my attempt to pay him a compliment—however, because he prefers the spot dances of swing, West Coast swing, and cha cha. In fact, he regularly drives three hours to dance with The Rebels, a swing club based in Chicago, returning home in the wee hours of the morning. He is a fan of the rhythm and blues music most often performed for West Coast swing, and he particularly enjoys engaging each song with different moves and punctuating steps.

As a guitarist and dance deejay, he spends more time collecting and listening to dance music than just about anyone else I know at the Regent. He is rivaled only by Leo, a retired physician who has set up his home computer to receive digital radio stations from California that play salsa, swing, and other dance genres around the clock. Leo has confessed that often he will sleep during the day so he can dance through the night in his living room when the reception is better. Both dancers enjoy ballroom dancing but deplore the staid quality of ballroom music, especially the "canned" synthesized arrangements, as Dean calls them.

Dean, who became one of my closest ballroom friends, is, in some ways, one of the most socially awkward men I have known. He is a bundle of nerves, with the ravaged GI tract to prove it. It took years for me to find my way in to him, to see his sweetness and his razor wit. And even then, it would occasionally dip behind a facade of aloofness, or he might disappear altogether for weeks at a time.

He has made it clear that he would like to have a girlfriend, or at least to experience a first kiss, but he also struggles to reveal himself to others. So, he dances. His way of connecting. His way of experiencing joy. Sometimes, I want to shake him, to rouse him from his fear and show him how lovable he is. But we never get so close. Instead, we dance.

The song concludes and couples wind down on the floor. At this point the ballroom is warm, and faces are flushed with perspiration and adrenalin. Dean excuses himself to change his shirt, which is drenched with sweat, and several dancers, men and women, cool themselves with their collapsible paper fans.

I take a break, heading first to the bar, which lies on the wall opposite the deejay table, to chat up Toby, tonight's bartender. Toby has already worked a full day as a piano technician, but he enjoys the dance crowd. A dancer himself, Toby is somewhat shy, so tending bar helps him to meet people. Besides, he likes David and likes helping out. Ballroom dancers rarely drink more than a few glasses of wine, preferring soft drinks and lots of water. This makes for lousy tips but an easy night of work. Tonight, however, there is a salsa dance following the ballroom event. The bar will be hopping by 11:30, and so Toby must double-check the stock of hard liquor and be sure the kegs are tapped, the garnishes prepped, and the ice stocked.

He takes a break to watch the hustle dancers with me. The song is a newer, fast-paced techno arrangement of a classic disco tune and a new addition to David's catalog. The crowd on the floor thins to no more than two-dozen couples for the physically demanding dance. I know from dancing with Toby that he doesn't mind the hustle, necessarily, but prefers the traditional smooth dances. He is currently working on the Viennese waltz, one of the most difficult genres. "But I can only spin in one direction. I don't know how to get turned around. Before I can even make it once around the floor, I get too dizzy and have to stop," he says in his typical self-deprecating way. "I'll get it eventually. You should practice with me though," he says. I vow to work on it with him at the Tuesday evening practice dance, and we do spend a number of weeks working on the Viennese waltz together. It feels a bit funny to dance with Toby, as if his shoulders do not line up with his hips. He and I both have issues with our core and moving from the center, an important component of couple dancing, especially for the traveling dances like the waltz. Together, quickly spinning only ever in one direction, I imagine we make quite a sight hurling down the floor barely in control. We never do get it.

I let Toby get back to work, knowing I'll catch him later tonight at David's, and head to the lobby to check in with Genevieve, who is enduring a bit of gentle ribbing about her New Jersey accent. She is not a dancer and has mixed feelings about her job at the Regent. Her primary responsibility is to manage the banquet aspect of the business—almost every Saturday the Regent hosts a wedding reception for which she is solely responsible—but she also tends the books for the dance classes and works the door for many of the dances. She loves the people she meets here, but the hours are inconvenient—late afternoons and evenings, later on Friday nights, and all day Saturday for the receptions. The job is not quite full-time, and as such, they do not offer healthcare benefits, although she thinks they might consider it soon. But the real issue is that she is anxious to have a career in hotel and restaurant management. This job is great training but does not offer long-term possibilities. Many of the young women to hold this position have moved on after a number of years to middle-management positions at large hotel chains, as will Genevieve soon enough.

The rotating crew of young women at the front desk is the source for a low undercurrent of jokes on the part of dancers as they mingle in the lobby. A few seem annoyed by the disruption of always having to work with "a new girl." David and Ellen do not seem to mind the turnover, even though it means having to train new help regularly. They both admit to liking the fresh ideas and the change that a new office administrator brings; it keeps their work from getting boring.

I find Genevieve looking over the photo board in the lobby, reviewing pictures from last week's Halloween masquerade dance. As she sees me turn the corner, she laughs freely, pointing to the one of me in a toga dancing with a mummy. "I can't believe these costumes," she says. I feel the same way. I am surprised by the number of people who dress up and the lengths to which they go. As for myself, I haven't worn a Halloween costume since I was a kid, and to this day I have not except for the Halloween dances at the Regent. I'm not usually such a joiner, and I cannot explain it. Finding a costume to dance in proves a bit of a challenge. My record is not too bad—a toga, a barmaid, a sixties go-go dancer, a flapper—these were fine enough. I am fairly certain that the mummy regretted his choice when he realized he had no peripheral vision and could barely breathe.

Sam arrives, smiling his easy smile, pays his six bucks to Genevieve, and together we walk back to the ballroom. My relationship with Sam is unlike my relationship with the rest of the dancers in that Sam is a former boyfriend of mine from a few years ago. He did not dance when I met him, had never danced. A thirty-something tennis coach, he struck a bargain with me that he would teach me how to play tennis and I would teach him how to dance. My performance in tennis classes was uninspired to say the least, and I have not picked up a racket since the days of our amicable split. Sam, on the other hand, took to dancing quickly, advanced far in a short time, and today is one of the most successful salsa dance teachers in the area. He is particularly fond of the swing—lindy, actually—salsa, and Latin genres, and he has become a key figure in organizing other dance events in town—a swing night at the local campus bar and a weekly salsa class and dance on the campus of the University of Illinois. He has competed regularly with several different partners.

As an athlete and a top-ranking tennis pro in the state, Sam considers competition a natural element of dance. He is accustomed to training for events, to long practices, and to giving attention to the smallest of details that cumulate in a winning performance. "Ballroom is like tennis this way," he says, as we watch foxtrotters circle the floor.

In fact, he and David have bartered a deal for lessons—Sam coached David and his son in tennis, and in exchange, David coached Sam in ballroom. David prefers these types of arrangements when possible, not as much for the financial benefits but for the networking opportunities and greater feeling of connection it fosters with clients. David is also a member of several local business and social organizations—the small business association, the rotary club, the Chinese community organization, the country club—and barters any number of arrangements with individuals from these different groups.

David follows the foxtrot with one of my favorite West Coast (triple) swings, Natalie Cole's version of "This Will Be (An Everlasting Love)." My singing along with the song encourages Sam to take my hand, and we head out to the floor. Of all the dances, I lament that my West Coast swing is not better. I find it difficult to settle into the music enough to engage my torso, hips, knees, or ankles.

As someone who loves to sing along to the music (taboo!), I especially appreciate it when David plays soul and R&B songs for West Coast swings. The rhythmic ambiguity of the dance mirrors the liquid nature of the vocals, and the convention of playful improvisation by both lead and follow make it particularly exhilarating when the right song is danced to with the right partner. Sam is such a partner, and we laugh as we both explore, and blunder, new variations of familiar moves, and surprise each other with interesting punctuations of the rhythm.

Tonight we hit it, and as Natalie approaches her climax, the long, winding up phrase "hugging and squeezing and kissing and pleasing, and oooooh oh . . ." Sam leads me in a series of fast spins—our own winding up of sorts. I am as weightless as I will ever be right now. Leveraging my fingers against Sam's over my head, the subtle increase of pressure in my fingers lets him know that I am going to take a few more turns to synchronize with the break of the phrase. The synchrony for these fast spins is tight: the feedback is immediate. There is no fudging this moment or I will fall out of this spin. We must be connected. We are right now, and we are both thrilled. As the song closes, we laugh and hug, walking off the floor to the quiet applause of a few friends who caught the synergy. I am sweaty, thirsty, and happy. The fatigue I felt when I arrived home from work earlier in the evening is gone, and at this moment I can't remember what tired feels like. My face literally aches from smiling so much this evening.

By the time the introduction to Tony Braxton's "Let It Flow" reaches me at the water fountain, Dean has taken my hand for the Nightclub two-step that cues the break to follow. I walk into his arms without hesitation, feeling his torso with my own before setting up our frame. The slow, romantic dance is a favorite because it stands apart from most of the other genres. Besides being genuinely romantic, as opposed to the more theatrical romanticism of the rumba, it is relatively simple, and there are fewer codified restrictions for moves and movement. More so than for any other dance, the music suggests it is a time to relax. Nevertheless, most couples flurry around us like whirlwinds, spinning and running to complete their favorite moves. The largest tempest of all, Dean and I loop around and through the other couples, in a style quite akin to the quickstep we performed earlier in the night. It seems almost comical, and though I enjoy the dance very much, I chuckle at the difference between this and the stationary rocking customary of slow dancing in other contexts, like the slow sway of a "buckle polisher" during a night of country two-step, my favorite of all couple dances.

I am reminded of one Sunday night earlier this summer at the Rose Bowl, a local country bar, when I was watching slow dancers sway in place, sweaty cheek to sweaty cheek, hands in the back pocket of the other's blue jeans. Cecil, a twenty-five-year-old engineering student and ballroom dancer, said with a tone of disgust, "I don't know what the point of that is." He was somewhat disappointed because he wanted to dance the Nightclub two-step, but knew there wasn't enough space to do so with the other couples glued to their spot on the floor. Having performed country dancing for years before I found myself in a ballroom, I was surprised by this comment. Half joking, I replied, "Cecil, that can be wonderful!" William chimed in, with a smile in his voice, "Cecil, that is the point of all other dancing!" Cecil remained unconvinced, so I took his hand and led him to the floor for a slow dance—a "Ramada Inn special" as David calls it, or "to polish our belt buckles" as it was called, tongue in cheek, by my country dance partners. Even though he refused to collapse his frame enough to bring me closer to him, Cecil's face still flushed with embarrassment and his nervous chatter drowned out the lyrics. I could tell he was simply biding his time until decorum allowed him to sit down.

Years later my boyfriend and future husband will accompany me to the Regent on my birthday. Given his lack of dance skills, we will break with local convention, take a place in the middle of the floor for my birthday waltz, and dance our own slow dance, slowly swaying to the music with full contact from shoulders to hips, while other celebrants waltz around us. The gesture will surprise and move our fellow dancers, for only true love, they believed, would motivate two individuals to essentially "not dance" for a ballroom audience.

Our Nightclub two-step over, Dean dances me to the water fountain where we began, a gesture I appreciate because my feet are killing me, and he has saved me a long walk from one end of the dance hall to the other to get a drink and talk some more with Toby as he tends the bar.

The Regent Ballroom and Banquet Center in Savoy, Illinois, with its newly renovated facade, 2005. Photo by the author.

Ellen Lin (left) and David Lin pose with the author. Photograph by Christopher Scales.

David Lin's class notes and mini-disc for his West Coast swing class. Photograph by the author.

Couples learning connection in class. In this instance, the leaders (men) are inviting their partner to move toward them, experimenting with the appropriate position of the left arm and hand, and how much pressure to employ to "invite" without "forcing." Followers (women) are learning how to balance the energy initiated by the leader and step forward without anticipating the lead. Photograph by Mark Nye.

Couples in class prepare to move forward in closed position for a lesson in American smooth. Notice that all the couples are facing in the same direction. For all of his classes, Lin stipulates the direction couples (and individuals) will face, as well as the direction and timing of their movement. While it may seem rigid to an outsider, dancers suggested they appreciated having all of these decisions made for them. The resultant parallel synchrony between all the dancers in the space was also effective for teaching floorcraft and generating group affinity. Photograph by Mark Nye.

David Lin and his teaching assistant Liz Meadows demonstrate closed position in class. Photograph by Mark Nye.

David Lin discussing the importance of frame. Photograph by the author.

Couples learning frame. This alternate arm position is used to help dancers learn how to define and maintain their frame, that is, the space within their arms and body. Leaders (men) and followers (women) are equally responsible for maintaining the integrity of their frame. Connection breaks down if one of the dancing couple collapses their frame. Photograph by author.

Couple practices the basic tango lunge during class. Photograph by the author.

Couple moving in closed position. Notice the look of concentration on the leader's face as he works through an extended pattern (sequence of steps) with his partner during class. Photograph by Mark Nye

Dancing couple in open position at a Friday night dance. In this moment, they face the wall of mirrors and can check their line and position. Photograph by Mark Nye.

Friday night dance. Changes to the lighting and seating arrangement of their classroom space cue participants to the different social frame and conventions of a Friday night dance. Photograph by Mark Nye.

Dancing couple enjoys a moment during a Friday night dance. Photograph by Mark Nye.

3

Bringing Coherence to the Sensuous Life

CONNECTION AND PARTNERSHIP AMONG SOCIAL DANCERS

Before the start of a Tuesday night practice dance, I was sitting with Dan and Mai, a retired academic couple of Japanese descent. The couple has been dancing for decades and has become a fixture on the dance floor. In their notable affection for one another, their playful, energetic synchrony, and their deep compatibility on and off the floor, they more aptly personify the American ideal of the romantic dancing couple even better than Fred and Ginger. Everyone knows them, and most admire their good fortune to each have found a marriage partner with whom they love to dance. "We started dancing back in the eighties," Mai began. Dan finished, "I had a heart attack, and my doctor told me I needed to exercise." "Then we quit for a while," Mai continued, "but we eventually came back and have been dancing ever since." I have watched the couple dance for years, and I never would have guessed that there was a time when their enthusiasm for the activity had waned. "Why did you quit?" I asked.

After a long pause, Mai responded, "Because a feminist shouldn't be led around by a man!" I had trouble reading the smiling twinkle in her eye, which seemed a contradiction to the indignant tone in her voice. "So, what changed? He still leads doesn't he?" I responded. "Well," she paused, "we missed it. So now I tell myself that I *allow* him to lead me." I would have preferred to continue the discussion, but the music started, and before I could even say "Thanks," Mai was dragging Dan onto the dance floor.

In 1985 John Blacking wrote, "Performances of dance frequently reflect and reinforce existing ideas and institutions, but they can also stimulate the imagination and help to bring coherence to the sensuous life, the 'intelligence of feeling,' which in turn can affect motivation, commitment, and decision making in other spheres of social life" (65). In this discussion of ballroom partnership and the lead-and-follow convention, I suggest that ballroom dance provided an opportunity to bring coherence to the sensuous life, a coherence that is tested by the contradictory expectations placed upon Regent dancers as middle-class, heterosexual men and women in twenty-first-century America.

In some ways, the opening vignette above distills the perplexing issue of gender in ballroom dance. We hear Mai's regret that the genre preserves the antiquated and regrettable gender discrimination that feminists have been attempting to dismantle for the last century and beyond. But we also hear a strong, outspoken woman reveling in an activity she loves to do. We hear an educated woman re-signifying her conventional role in order to declare her own will, power, and right to move in ways that make her feel good, and perhaps more intriguing, we hear very little from her husband at all. The ballroom is populated by women who work, as Mai does, to balance the pressure to be strong, independent women on the one hand, and on the other, to live and move in a social world that feels great ambivalence about strong, independent women. Here we find heterosexual women learning how to balance their own rights and freedoms while also creating healthy, interdependent relationships in which they can thrive. And perhaps, most relevant for the purposes of the story I am weaving, we hear women trying to understand how to be beautiful in strength and independence in light of a legacy of feminine beauty tied to frailty and weakness.

Here too, are heterosexual men, struggling with the instability of white, middle-class masculinity in twenty-first-century America. While at some level they understand and no doubt capitalize on their privileged position, they also seek to create equitable relationships with the women in their lives, many of them equals in terms of sociocultural and socioeconomic status. In vulnerable moments they reveal a great deal of discomfort about American gender politics, as if the lines of appropriate behavior shift from day to day, moment to moment. They also struggle with the gendered nature of dance. Many conceal their interest in dancing from friends and family for fear of ridicule and of having their manhood called into question. They choose to sublimate their own love of dancing into an obligation they fulfill solely for their wives or as a promise made to a physician. They wonder, with sweaty palms and trembling arms, how they can lead when they feel so inept. For these dancers, it is generally taken for granted that dancing couples are heterosexual in nature, but in this post-women's-rights era still very deeply influenced by Victorian ideals, how men and women should relate to one another is often unclear.

Ballroom dance is one place where individuals work out the tensions between the inherited legacy of sexism and the desire for a more equitable future. It is a place that helps them bring coherence to this push-and-pull experience. In a "separate but equal" framework, the genre stipulates gender segregation in the form of the male lead / female follow convention while simultaneously fostering notions of equality and women's rights to claim authority in the dancing couple. Men learn to move in ways that sometimes feel effeminate in order to become strong leaders in the service of women and their own aesthetic experience. Furthermore, the genre fertilizes heterosexually normative notions of ideal female physical beauty as an accessory to and signifier of her partner's prowess, while also celebrating her own athleticism and physical strength. Performance of the genre inscribes, in one moment, a contradictory experience in which social norms for gendered identities are both upheld and transgressed—a "back and forth" similar to that discussed by anthropologist and dance scholar Jonathan Skinner in his analysis of salsa dancers in the British Isles (2008).

Ballroom dance provides an opportunity for dancers to move, literally, within and between these expectations, fusing them into one coherent aesthetic experience (see also Spiller 2010). Exploring the power of movement, one's own physicality, athleticism, beauty, and grace, the power to please a partner and an audience as well as oneself, are wrapped into a dense, meaningful moment—visceral, aesthetic, intimate, and social. As such, ballroom dance is rich in symbolic resources. Synchrony is mysterious: this is part of its appeal. It is also what makes it open to interpretation, a site of constant framing and reshaping. Such discursive frames are constitutive of experience and part of the affective potential of dance relationships.

What I am suggesting here is not that performance is reflective of a coherent understanding of dancers' own gendered subject position. Nor am I suggesting that the conventions of ballroom dance encompass a logical, singular concept with regard to gender. Rather, I propose that through performance they create a discrete and singular, if not coherent, experience through which they wrestle with the incoherent, inconsistent reality of gender. In his study of Zulu migrants in South Africa, Veit Erlmann suggests something similar when he states, "Examination of a performance tradition such as isicathamiya suggests . . . that the use of complex and heterogeneous symbols which continually pull the anthropologist into ever wider, polycentric hermeneutic circles is itself a performative strategy" (1992, 689). Erlmann encourages us to move away from constructing narratives of coherent performance styles or closed, logical systems of meaning, suggesting that scholars accept the challenge embodied in the discrepancies and disjunctures of performance.

Nowhere is this more imperative than in the analysis of American couple dancing; for gender as experienced, especially in this context, is itself riddled with discrepancies and disjunctures. Gender on the conceptual level is "a selective set of idealized, normative qualities attributed to sexuality, used as an instrument of power that produces inequalities and dependencies" (Morris 1995, 578). These qualities are enacted in performance, as Judith Butler has noted in her famous quip, "All of gender is drag" (1999). Although gender exists only in performance, we fabricate the idea that these performative acts are expressive of an interiority—an inner core identity—that does not necessarily exist. "In other words, acts and gestures, articulated and enacted desires create the illusion of an interior and organizing gender core, an illusion discursively maintained for the purposes of the regulation of sexuality within the obligatory frame of reproductive heterosexuality" (177). These performances are crucial acts in the creation of gendered subject formation. In the process of performance, normative ideals are prescribed on/in/through/with/by the body.[1]

These normative ideals, however, reside in an uneasy relationship to the experience and ongoing performance of gender. For middle- and upper-class American women at least, gender, albeit a fabrication based in the selective maintenance of certain characteristics, exists at the conceptual level as well as the performative. That is, as educated elites, ballroom dancers know gender—in a critical, even academic sense—as an arbitrary fabrication and instrument of discrimination while they simultaneously believe that it is, in fact, essentially and biologically determined, at least to some degree. The contradictory understandings inform the ways in which individuals experience gender on a day-to-day, moment-to-moment basis.

The concept of gender as an illusory core set of ideal thoughts and behaviors does not unilaterally drive the everyday performance of gender, nor does experience determine the conceptual model. Rather, the four components mentioned here—conceptual categories and experience, gender as fabrication, and gender as essential—exist in an uneasy and contradictory quagmire, riddled with discrepancies and inconsistencies. The performance of ballroom dance serves as a dialectic that resides at their intersection. When I asked Joy, a PhD and full faculty member in the sciences, and her academic spouse, both white, how it felt to ballroom dance, she responded with embarrassment. Hanging her head and flushed red in the cheeks, she said, "I know it's wrong, but I feel like a princess. Like a beautiful princess." Like many of her fellow dancers, she felt compelled to ground the feeling of dance in the language of gender (and class to some degree) while also communicating gesturally that she understood gender to be an analytically and socially complicated identity construct. Also heard in her comment is a sense that she feels obligated to toe some sort of feminist line, which is in conflict with the enjoyment derived from performing what she perceives to be a sexist stereotype.

Liz Friedlander, director of the feature film *Take the Lead*, starring Antonio Banderas, feels the same way. She confesses that dancing with Banderas's real-life counterpart, ballroom dance teacher Pierre Dulaine, is "enough to temporarily make a lady delight in being treated as such, no matter how outdated the custom may seem. I'm very much a strong woman. I'm working, I'm in control," recalls Friedlander. "I danced the tango with Pierre and he lifted me, and I was just, like, [gasp]. You get this girl thing rushing to you. It puts you in touch with things that you almost intellectualize out of yourself and it's just fun'" (Henerson 2006).

Both of these examples suggest that ballroom dance might serve as a kind of transgressive act in the classic "pressure release valve" model associated with carnival, but in an unconventional way. In this instance, the daily lives of the women I worked with contravened traditional American gender values. As business owners, bosses, scientists, doctors, lawyers, and professionals of all sorts, their lives were a testament to a new postfeminist reality for American women. On a very personal level, however, they continued to wrestle with the ramifications of such actions in their larger social world. Regardless of how successful such women can be, Americans nevertheless feel a great deal of ambivalence about them. The women I worked with felt some ambivalence as well, for they struggled on a daily basis with the consequences of flouting traditional gender expectations. Ballroom dance provided them the opportunity to perform more conventional femininity, violating the sensibilities of feminism without the social costs associated with doing so. They could play the part of the beautiful princess, or experience what Friedlander called "this girl thing," in the isolated context of the ballroom without sacrificing the social power they have earned in their professional lives by shunning those very same notions.

Through ballroom dance, individuals employ an incoherent set of symbolic resources—signifiers with the potential for multiple and conflicting meanings—through which they stimulate their imaginations and "help to bring coherence to the sensuous life." The subsequent sections in this chapter introduce some of the symbolic resources that compose ballroom dance and the ways dancers derive meaning—often multiple, discordant, and incongruous—from its performance.

To Lead and Follow

From the very first dance class, the terms men and leaders were coterminous, and much of the class time at the Regent was dedicated to the lead technique. To my knowledge, no one ever challenged the division of leaders and followers into men and women, and never in my time there did a same-sex couple attempt to enroll in Regent classes. If they had, I suspect they would have been turned away.[2]

As the leader, the man was responsible for choosing the sequence of moves, initiating those moves, and guiding the woman through them. He was expected to gauge the abilities of his partner and lead only moves that were appropriate to her skill level (or perhaps slightly higher). The leader was also responsible for "floor craft," which involves guiding the couple across the floor in relationship to the physical space and other couples, and making sure that he avoids collision with other dancers, chairs, support beams, and the like.

A disproportionate amount of class time in the beginning courses is invested in teaching the men to lead. The basic introduction to the lead technique involves a series of exercises and metaphors to explain the art of leading and of connection, literally connecting with one's partner. The most commonly used exercise was to have the couple stand facing one another, open palms held out vertically at chest height, touching those of their partner to resemble a children's clapping game. With elbows fixed in position, the leader is then asked to step forward and, if performed correctly, his partner will feel his body move forward and step backwards. Encouraging them to try it over again, David jokes, "Keep those arms flexed—we don't want spaghetti arms!" As students begin to understand the nature of the exercise, he suggests that the key "is remembering to take your body with you." He offers an example to clarify. "When you go to the grocery, and you have a cart full of food, you don't push with your arms and feet and leave your backside behind, right? Of course not. You lean into the cart with your body first to get the cart moving and then engage the arms and feet to keep it moving and guide its direction." Students try this exercise with several partners in the class. As the men are beginning to learn the premise of leading from the body, he turns his attention to the women. "Ladies, wait for his lead. Don't anticipate, and don't let your elbows move behind your body. They should stay right there at your side." David then turns his attention to the hands. "Your palms should be open. No gripping, gentlemen!" The students repeat this exercise a few more times, changing partners upon David's request, before putting what they have learned about connection into practice with an actual waltz step.

The lead for the basic step of any ballroom genre requires little arm movement. Couples assume the closed position characteristic of the genre and remain in this position throughout the performance of the basic step. In this context, leading from the body to guide one's partner around the dance floor is crucial. Any kind of variation from the basic, however, requires signals with the arms and hands as well as the body. At this point in the class, couples separate to opposite sides of the floor, and the teacher breaks down the arm movements and connects them to the rhythm of the footwork. "Gentlemen," David instructs for the swing underarm turn, "when your left foot hits count one, your left arm should be raised over your left shoulder. On the second slow step, your right hand applies gentle pressure on her back to guide her under her own arm, and then on the quick step you bring your arm back down in front of you." After leading the women through their part in similar fashion, couples reunite to try the step slowly and without music, while the teacher counts out loud.

Much of the class time in the early courses is dedicated to learning the men's parts. Women were taught their steps and guided on some of the rudimentary skills necessary for good dancing and good following. In the early stages, women learn how to "trust a leader"—waiting for the lead rather than anticipating on her own; learning the appropriate amount of pressure necessary in the shoulders, arms, and hands; learning how to move without looking down at her feet, and how to move backwards without looking over her shoulder. It is not until the more advanced levels, however, that more detail is offered on the follow technique. Difficult issues, such as balance, momentum, and center, are introduced only in the intermediate classes, after both men and women have mastered the basic steps and some rudimentary knowledge of lead and follow.

Unlike other cultural groups that employ strictly segregated contexts for the performance of music and dance, there are no mysterious, restricted realms of maleness and femaleness. Men and women attended the same classes and learn their parts in the same social space. So while the division of labor in the couple is segregated, each is privy to the lessons of the other. It is not uncommon to see women following along with the lesson for the lead part and, to a lesser degree, to see the men learning the follow part, even though it is understood that they probably would never perform these roles at a dance event. Men and women have access to the same information, can attend to it as was their prerogative, and are introduced to the challenges posed by each part.

The Regent classes did not accommodate cross-gendered performance. While women were free to follow along with the lead lesson, they were not allowed to join the rotation of men in order to practice the part with a (female) follower. David suggests that to do so would be problematic. He requires his students to rotate partners, and in so doing they must dance with every member of the opposite sex in the room. Were a woman to join the rotation of men, every woman in attendance would be required to dance with her. David has remarked, "Surely some people won't have a problem with this, but others might. I know I would. I don't want to dance with a guy. If it happens often enough, [my students] will either complain to me or simply stop showing up and I've lost my customers."

Other ballroom teachers, and especially those who promote participation in competition, encourage their more advanced students to perform the part of the opposite sex in class; in the Dancing Illini practice dances, for example, it was not remarkable to see two members of the same sex practicing as a couple. For Regent dancers, the genre was not only iconic of heterosexual relationships, it was indexical of them as well (Lea 2001; Peirce 1955; Turino 1999). That is, through the materiality of man and woman dancing together did Regent dancers realize the experience they sought—being in synchrony with another in a way that held the potential for feeling beautiful. The predominantly heterosexual dancers I worked with were not socialized to think it was even possible to become beautiful with members of the same sex.[3]

Reframing Gender and Restructuring Power

Given the male-lead/female-follow convention, it is tempting to reduce the genre to an expression of patriarchal dominance, outing the hegemonic role of male leaders who control in a very real sense the bodies and experiences of the women in their lives. Rather, I would like to move beyond the rules of the genre to how they work in practice, introducing some of the ways men and women dancers operate within this structural framework to create a different kind of power arrangement. It does not render the patriarchal power of the male-lead/female-follow convention impotent, but these strategies do work against the hegemonic potential inherent in them.

One strategy that both female and male Regent dancers employed to minimize the inherent discrimination of the male-lead/female-follow convention was to reframe the way the relationship was understood. Rather than leading or forcing, dancers preferred to consider the role of the man to invite. As several dancers (men and women) told me, "The man doesn't make a woman do anything; he invites her to perform a move. If she wants to, she does it. If not, she doesn't." While this narrative was always a part of David's teaching of the lead/follow relationship, I noticed he made more frequent and explicit references to it during my follow-up trip to the region in 2005, and his students followed suit.

This reframing of the relationship had real consequences, and women spoke often of their refusal to dance in ways they did not find pleasurable. In some instances they simply refused to dance certain genres with certain partners, a very common strategy, or they attempted to reconcile the differences verbally or otherwise. For example, Iris related this story about a disagreement she had regarding how a move was to be led,

> A lot of times I would just, . . . I don't want to hurt anybody's ego so a lot of times I'll be like, "That didn't work out right. One of us isn't doing this right, so let's keep working on it." I'm open to the possibility that I'm the one doing it wrong, but if I've done it before . . . I mean look, there are certain moves, like the underarm turn in the rumba, this guy tried to tell me I was doing it wrong and I know I was right, and he said, "That's how everyone else does it." And I said, "Well, that's not how I do it."

Another context in which this refiguring of gender relationships had real consequences related to timing and dancing to music. For reasons I will discuss in the following section, most women felt very confident in their musical ability relative to their male counterparts, and most told me that they refused to dance "off-time" with a partner. "If he doesn't feel the rhythm, then I will ground it, but I will not dance off-time. It's just wrong," stated Joy in commenting on dancing with her rhythmically challenged husband (who was sitting beside her as she spoke). Or as Jane remarked, "I'll just say 'Can we stop for a moment?' and then take the opportunity to signal the rhythm with my body. He may not even be aware that that's what's happening." This trend, of women grounding the rhythm or refusing to dance off-time was also a new component of the follow technique as taught at the Regent. In talking with me about the shift, David stated his reasons for this were musical. "One of the things I learned from having salsa dances here is how important the music is. I had never thought about it. I always loved to dance and never really cared about the music much. But some of the salsa music is so, . . . [he begins to dance] you just move. I decided that the music, and making sure my students can really hear it, is very important. So I have started opening my classes with rhythm exercises and I spend more time talking about the music. Now I push them to dance on time, and many times that means that the woman has to ground the rhythm. They just seem to be able to hear it better; they seem more relaxed." While his motives may have been purely musical, David's decision to empower women to ground the rhythm of the dancing couple had made a significant impact in the three years I was away. Signaling this trend was Jane, one of David's instructors, who was surprised to hear that another studio taught otherwise:

> I think that a woman is always responsible for her balance, and so is the man. A woman is also responsible for the rhythm, and so is the man. I have heard that [another instructor] told his classes that if the man danced off-time, the woman danced off-time. I was like, "Uh uh, no." You cannot expect that. That is not a fair arrangement. I mean, I don't think I can dance off-time unless somebody is just absolutely holding on to me so tight that I can't move! But I think that rhythm is responsibility for both partners. And sometimes if one partner has a stronger sense of rhythm, which is often the case in social dances, then they anchor the rhythm. Plus, in the beginning, men have so much to think about because they're not just dancing their own part, but they have to think about the leads, the signals, the timing of it, and they have to know what step they're doing next. They definitely have more to deal with than the woman does [in the] beginning. But that often causes them to lose sense of the music. Even if they can hear it when you just stand there and clap, they can't hold on to it when they've got so many other things to think about—they lose it. So it can really help to dance with a partner who can help them.

Women in beginning and intermediate levels often assumed this kind of authority on the grounds that they were the more competent dancer of the couple. Competence is an important structuring component in dance relationships and can be demonstrated in a number of areas, including virtuosity as a dancer in general, familiarity with the particular genre being performed at the moment, and the ability "to hear music." While it was possible at the Regent for both men and women to achieve advanced competence, beginners often generalized that women were the more competent, as David implied himself when discussing women's superior ability to hear music. In my experience with dancing couples—beginning and intermediate dancers—men and women alike were more likely to acknowledge, if not genuinely overestimate, the abilities of the woman, while those of the man were under constant private and public scrutiny. In the early years of dancing, women assumed an authority that was articulated in a number of ways, including subtle nonverbal corrections to the posture or positioning of her partner; explicit criticism of the performance just completed; stopping in the middle of a move to suggest that the lead is not right; soliciting the help of a more advanced dancer or teacher; counting aloud or gesturing when to begin the step; and leading from the follow position, often called "backleading" or "hijacking moves."

There are several interrelated reasons for this. First, women generally feel much more at ease in the very early stages of dancing. After all, in most American contexts, dancing has been constructed as a women's activity, and the ballroom has historically been a female space (Aldrich 1991; Cook 1998; Wagner 1997). Most male ballroom dancers who spoke with me experienced at least some emotional, psychological, social, or physical barriers to accepting themselves as dancers. Many testified that they were so embarrassed or insecure that they did not share the fact that they were studying dance with their friends, co-workers, or extended families until they had achieved some degree of success. Brett's story is common among single men:

JB: What do you do actually?

B: I'm a contractor. That's the other thing. I'm essentially a construction worker, I own a construction company and I work with construction workers, and so if my grammar slips that's why, because I'm around those guys all the time.

JB: That's ok, I'm from a family of mechanics. I get it.

B: Yeah, you know. I fish and do all that stuff. I'm a guy. So it's a pretty bizarre thing to take a dance class. In fact, I didn't tell anyone for a long time. I would just say I was busy on Monday nights, but I wouldn't tell 'em what I was doing. But then I went to a wedding reception, and it became obvious what I had been doing in my spare time.

JB: So there were lots of construction workers at the reception?

B: Some were, some just knew me, some were customers, and they found out I knew how to dance, and it was like, "Hey where did you learn how to do that?"

JB: How did you feel at that moment?

B: It was very empowering. I can tell you, now that I think about it, I went to a wedding reception last Saturday, and now there is no way I would [not dance]. [Before I started ballroom dancing,] I probably only danced six times in my life prior to that. I mean, I capitulated. My wife would want to dance and I would get up and dance, you know, the way people dance at those things. But now there is no way. It [the dance floor] would have to be full to keep me from getting out there. Now I have no problem being the only person out there. And that happened three or four times that I was the only one out there on the floor and I would never have thought of doing that before. But now I'm empowered. I can do this. It's no big deal. It's kinda good. Not only is it good, it's a rush, in a way, to be able to do that.

Women, on the other hand, testified to childhood days spent dancing in their living rooms and aspirations of dancing that were never fully realized in their youth. In our discussions, they connected dancing to their other hobbies such as theater, music, aerobics, race walking, or ice dancing, and they made it clear that although they may not have danced their whole lives, they always considered themselves potential dancers—it was always present in their self-imaginary. Rather than a disjuncture from a previous, immobile, or non-artistic self, as many men attested, dancing was, for women, the completion or fulfillment of an identity they always felt, or at least hoped themselves to be capable of. Louise, for example, used to perform in an improvisational theater troupe in college, and she missed that outlet once she graduated. She found ballroom preferable to community theater because she liked being able to perform without being center stage. "Here you can show off and sometimes nobody is watching you. Sometimes your students might be, sometimes a few people, I suppose. It is fun to show off the little things, but it's more important to know that I know I'm performing and doing well with my partner. I'm not performing for anybody but me. It's a challenge and a puzzle."

This affinity for dance caused women to feel much more comfortable in the Regent ballroom and led to a much easier time acquiring basic competency. Simply put, they were generally less nervous and less distracted by their own anxiety. Furthermore, the learning curve for partnership dancing is frontloaded for men and backloaded for the women. In Regent class levels 1 through 3, men struggled to achieve even a moderate level of ability, while women more quickly felt the benefits of the lessons. Women, for example, were often allowed to skip a beginning course level, while men, on the other hand, were more often encouraged to repeat a beginning course level. Later, after level 4, the women were asked to reconsider aspects of following they initially took for granted—things like balance, momentum, line and so forth—that posed an added challenge. But the nature of ballroom performance allowed women to enjoy dancing to a great degree without ever addressing these concerns.

While their partners wrestled with their own anxiety and the logistics of leading, women felt more comfortable and were free to enjoy dancing as an aesthetic experience. They were free to engage the music, and in fact, if their partner struggled with hearing the music, they generally took charge of making sure they were dancing in time. For these reasons it was common for women to assume a leadership role within the dancing couple early on, one that served as a counterbalance to the hegemonic potential of the male-lead/female-follow convention. Each performance held the potential to both reinforce the existing institutional patriarchy and to re-inscribe it with a new gender dynamic wherein women led as well.

Reciprocity and Connection

Ballroom dance is rich in symbolic resources—dense layers of movement, from the barely perceptible closing of one finger to a major shift in direction of the dancing couple—as the movements unfold in quick succession and shift with every passing second like ocean waves. These movements are considered and conceptualized, verbalized and triggered by music, and they come to signify through an interesting and unfolding process of collective collaboration. As dancers develop their skills, they employ these resources in different ways and to different ends.

Up to this point I have focused on how beginning and intermediate dancers at the Regent understood their roles and abilities as leader and follower. Dancers with a high level of ability and investment in the genre, however, framed them differently. Every advanced dancer and teacher with whom I worked framed the dance relationship as one of two equal partners; many likened it to a sports team. They concurred that the lead-and-follow techniques each pose different challenges and that neither gender has a distinct or inherent advantage over the other at the highest levels of performance. Both individuals have their role to play, and both are equally responsible for the success of the partnership. This is a lesson that students do eventually learn, but generally over a long period. Part of the process of learning to ballroom dance is to replace the culturally informed notion of follower as passive with one of more active engagement. Following and receiving, actions considered to be more passive and devalued in a society that privileges the more masculine-encoded actions of leading and asserting, can, in actuality, require a significant (and often greater) degree of attention, skill, and strength that remains unrecognized by society's dominant members.[4]

Advanced dancers sited the obligations that both dancers share. As William told me any number of times, "Look, each person has to carry their own weight, maintain their own balance, control their own momentum, and they have to know their steps. It's all tough." Furthermore, both are responsible for maintaining the "frame," the space created by the partner position, which is achieved through an active upper torso, shoulders, and arms, and an equal matching of pressure at points of contact. The mechanics of this dynamic is called "connection," and it is based on a particular kind of reciprocity and equality of competence, attention, pressure, and energy. Without a strong connection, there can be no successful lead and follow.

David emphasized that both individuals of a partnership are responsible for bringing to the dance equal energy, figuratively and literally. The mechanics of optimal lead and follow require each partner to apply equal pressure on points of contact (fingers, hands, arms, and shoulders are very important). In class, David asked couples to imagine that a sheet of paper was placed between the left hand of the man and the right of the woman. Partners needed to apply equal pressure to keep the paper from falling to the ground, but no more. The follower must push or pull with as much pressure as the leader, but it is not always the man who dictates this force; rather, it is negotiated between the couple through very subtle physical cues. David also stressed that each dancer must pay equal attention to the messages his or her partner is sending. He described the relationship to me this way: "The man invites the woman to perform a move, she accepts, and then he should follow her. It's like a conversation; you have to listen to each other. It doesn't matter who starts it, what matters is that you are listening."

Jane described the balance another way:

> I grew up riding horses. And I sometimes liken it to the relationship between a horse and rider. People might think that that also sounds sexist thinking of the man as the rider and the woman as the horse, but I think people who really love and understand horses know the respect and partnership between someone and a horse they love. It's fifty-fifty. It's a very strong partnership, a very strong relationship. And it's not, I mean, you do see riders who are harsh with their horses, you do see riders who over-lead them. But then you see others who really understand that relationship, and it takes so little. It takes so little to ask the horse. I lived out in the country and my father had grown up riding horses, and he, you know, brought a horse to me and I rode bareback. I didn't really get any technical riding lessons. I've taken a few recently and realized how complicated it can be, like the direction that you look affects the direction that your horse is going to go. But I did understand just from loving animals and loving horses that the relationship was fifty-fifty. The horse is just as just as important as the rider. I'm always very cautious to liken ballroom dancing to that, but if you understand the profound respect that I give the partnership between a horse and a rider, then you can know what I mean.

Experienced dancers cited connection as one of the most affective aspects of the genre. It is attributed with an almost magical quality, sometimes likened to an addictive drug, and it is what motivates most dancers I know to keep dancing. For instance, Matthew described it this way:

> What I look for in a partner, I guess, . . . I look for connection. There's the physical, the physical abilities of a person that they're able to dance. They have rhythm. There's a solid connection. There are some girls who feel like a Raggedy Ann doll. There's nothing there and you can't do anything with them.
>
> The other girls, you know it immediately when you get into dance position, you can ffffffeel the connection. You're both in tune with each other. You feel

> it here and here and here (pointing to his head, his torso, and his arms). Then there's the ineffable connection that you enjoy dancing with a person and you can see [she] enjoys dancing with you. [She] knows that you're enjoying [her], and you know that [she] knows that you know. You feel like you've been dancing with this woman forever.
>
> See, that's like heroin. It's just like crack. I look for those super dances—I get maybe one of these a year, possibly two. These dances are like crack. You start looking for them. You want another and another and you keep looking for them anywhere you can find them. And you can dance with a complete stranger and it's like you've been dancing together for ten years. The music is right, everything is completely right, and it works. It's dynamite."

David regularly admonished me about becoming too good a dancer. "It's lonely at the top. The better you are, the harder it is to find partners with whom you can really dance." To "really dance" is to find the kind of connection that makes for the most joyful, exciting, and magical of dance experiences. And while he was generally framing his comment as advice to me, I sensed that it was more often a lament about his own dancing life. As the best dancer in the region, David had no partners whose skills matched his own. As such, his opportunities for the kind of connection described above were limited.

Connection is based on equality and reciprocity in a number of forms, and an asymmetrical distribution of power is less than ideal. The best partnerships, those that make each dancer feel good and compatible with one another—the kind that Matthew chases and that Mai and Dan already have—are those in which both individuals are at the same level of competence and possess the same level of investment. They are equally strong in their skills and equally capable of challenging the other dancer to optimal performance. In my experience watching dancers develop their skills, people sought partnerships built upon connection and reciprocity, not upon their ability to assert dominance and authority.

That being said, the structural qualities of the lead/follow relationship are undeniable. Men assert their freedom and their will—choosing the moves, guiding the women's movement to a much greater degree than she his, and assuming a lion's share of the credit for strong performances. This inequality of partnership, when juxtaposed against the equality and reciprocity of connection, suggests the kind of incoherence that Blacking alludes to in the quote with which I opened this chapter. The sensuous life is riddled with inconsistencies, perhaps no more so than when it comes to gender.

As college-educated professionals, most of the dancers with whom I worked have had some exposure to the postmodern critique of gender in an academic setting or elsewhere. They have learned that, at some level, gender is a constructed notion, and that at least at the level of "political correctness," if not genuinely, it should be treated with care. But they have been socialized according to a conflicting set of gender expectations. While on one hand they understand that many gendered stereotypes are false, they also believe at some level that such stereotypes are an expression of "natural" differences between men and women. Perhaps most important, they know that there are still very real and tangible social repercussions for those who challenge/transgress/violate them, regardless of the stereotypes' actual validity.

Walking the line between some sort of ideal or more equitable gender arrangement and the reality of gender inequality is part and parcel of the everyday lived experiences for many middle-class Americans and was certainly true for the dancers I worked with. Furthermore, the issue of gender is a minefield that makes frank discussion about it tricky or awkward in general social situations. This is why the joking stance was the most popular way to approach the discussion of gender roles in ballroom dance, especially among male dancers. The position allows for one to express ambiguously, perhaps in hyperbole, something he or she might well believe on one hand to be true, while also calling into question the truth or validity of the statement with a wink and a smile.

Many antiquated ideas about gender, expressed and embodied in ballroom, were often stated with an ironic tone or a wink. For example, typically when I made a mistake, I was quick to apologize even though I understood it was unnecessary. When I did so, William, one of the most accomplished dancers in the area, would respond with a smile and a wink, "Don't worry about it. Everyone knows that any mistake is my fault [meaning, the fault of the leader]." It was both true and not true. There were at least three different interpretations of his utterance, and I think to some degree they were all intended simultaneously. To some extent the man, as leader, is responsible for a failed move, as it is his job to assess what his partner is capable of and to correctly lead moves appropriate to her abilities. If a move fails, he has misjudged something. But, in fact, failed dance moves are sometimes the fault of the follower, and William often offered his truism when, I think, he believed the woman was at fault. Finally, his statement expresses the kind of chivalric male/female relationships encoded in ballroom dance. Even if the woman is at fault, the man should assume the blame because it is courteous to do so. Dancers often suggest that the placement of blame should be irrelevant, but it rarely is.

Similarly, when introducing the notion of lead/follow to his beginner students, David countered the stereotypical notion of men dominating or bullying their partners. "You don't force the woman into a move, you invite her to perform it," he said, as he demonstrated his light touch on his partner. "But, be prepared," he smiled deviously. "She may turn you down!" At which point he broke into laughter and slapped his knee. To some degree, David believed in equality between dance partners. In this regard, he was not unlike most advanced and competition dancers, who perceived ballroom to be more a sport than a leisure activity, with the couple comprising two individuals performing different but equally important functions. His emphasis on the necessary equal pressure in couple position, and the stressing of the leader's role to invite rather than force his partner, was a genuine expression of his views about the couple dynamic. But the joking frame of the statement also evokes comical stereotypes of women, legitimating, in a way, the man's role as leader in the process. David invokes the conventional archetype of woman as unpredictable, precocious, and temperamental, while simultaneously also mocking the strong female who makes her will known.

While women also joked about the differences between the sexes, more often the topic arose within the context of life choices to be puzzled over. For even as they sought reciprocity in their dance experiences, the dancers with whom I worked, and especially the women, struggled with its parameters—how to understand it in light of a legacy of institutional misogyny and discrimination and their own obligations as a woman—to their community, to their partner and family, and to themselves. Their stories are telling—not to the degree that they are exceptional, but because they are so mundane. Examples include the evenings spent chatting with women in the Regent lobby about the pressure to wear high-heels even though they are painful, about how good it feels to dress up, and the guilty pleasures of sweat pants. There were talks with Sylvia, a successful real estate agent and divorced mother of adult children, who worried that marrying Jimmy would somehow impinge on the freedom and independence that she won through a painful divorce and years of living on her own; Louise, a thirty-six-year-old single professional spoke with regret about having chosen her job over a love lost years ago; and Marilyn, who swore that dance class was the only thing holding her marriage together. Learning when to lead and when to follow, when to push or pull, when to give or take, this is the stuff of everyday life as well as ballroom dance. Moving in synchrony with a partner of the opposite sex, dancing provides an embodied metaphor for the kinds of compromises these dancers make off the floor as well.[5]

The Princess Factor

Tucked away in the business offices of the Regent, I met with Marilyn, a white, middle-class, middle-aged social ballroom dancer in Savoy, Illinois, whose favorite dances were the rumba and salsa. The discussion was a long and emotional one, as was the often the case in my more formal one-on-one interviews. Through a conversation of dancing, I learned about her somewhat strained relationship with her husband, Arnold, a workaholic computer programmer and fellow ballroom dancer. A homeschooler who has wrestled with her decision to give up a work life outside of the home, Marilyn felt confined and stifled by her day-to-day life, and dancing provided a public venue for enjoyment, self-expression, and physical activity. I closed my interview with Marilyn as I did most of my formal interviews, by asking her to complete this sentence, "When I am dancing, I feel. . . ." Marilyn paused for a long time and then said, "like a princess." "How so?" I asked, and as she began to tear up she whispered, "For that moment, for that dance, while it's clicking, the world is mine. And I will turn into a pumpkin at the end of the dance and deal with my life."

As mentioned above, many women claimed that one of the most meaningful aspects of ballroom dance was that performing it made them feel beautiful like a princess, if even only for the duration of the dance. Perhaps it should not be surprising. The princess has served as the archetype of female beauty in myths, fables, and movies. Her connection to magic and stories of transformation further her potential as an iconic figure for the kind of transformative experience ballroom dancers claim to have when performing.

In an email discussion about the "princess factor," William, reminded me that it was also a factor for men as well:

> A second observation—the princess factor—(you quoted Joy as mentioning it)—is one of the common reasons that women enjoy the ballroom experience. Note that being a princess is one of those complex things—playing dress up, putting on the good manners, expecting to be treated like a princess, being treated like a princess. Note that having an admiring prince or two or three around improves the illusion as well. Men are also impacted by the princess factor. They act differently when dressed up—with even minor changes in expected dress (for example, a dress code that states "no blue jeans") yielding results. Men act differently toward women in the princess role—even if the woman is familiar to them.

While no men suggested that they felt they became a beautiful prince through dance, William is correct in suggesting that they, too, experience something akin to the "princess factor," most often coded with the world "gentleman." For instance, Brett thought ballroom dancing was the culmination of becoming a "gentleman":

> JB: When did you start dancing?
>
> B: I started about five years ago. I've taken Ballroom 1 and 2, Salsa and Nightclub two-step, and personally I take every class twice.

JB: The same class twice?

B: Mmmhmm. Same class twice, regardless. Cuz to me it's like watching a movie twice, every time you watch a movie you get [something else out of it.]

JB: So you're not bored?

B: Actually it feels better because the second time I might look like I actually know what I'm doing, and the first time I'm out in left field.

JB: I'm sure your partners appreciate that.

B: It is funny how the women like to see me come around because they know I have a pretty good idea what I'm doing now because this is round two for me. The other thing, too, I think we got off the subject a little, my mom is a big proponent of dancing and used to preach to us all the time and we had little classes at home I remember every prom and every homecoming [I had] to dance with my mom before I could leave the house. I did all the things she thought were important, but I never took any dance classes of any kind until I was or thirty-five or thirty-six, I guess, so that was the culmination of being a gentleman, learning how to dance.

Like the princess, the gentleman also serves as an archetype of gender rooted in a particular class disposition. Gentlemen and princesses are literal or figurative nobility. Becoming a princess is about becoming a particular type of beautiful, affluent woman. Similarly, becoming a gentleman is about becoming a particular brand of handsome and affluent man. Performing ballroom dance is often accredited with the potential to cultivate such ennoblement (Malnig 1997).

My last fieldwork stint took place shortly after the release of *Mad Hot Ballroom*, a documentary film about a pilot program to introduce children from three of New York City's inner-city schools to ballroom dance. As the film's synopsis reads, "Told from their candid, sometimes hilarious perspectives, these kids are transformed, from reluctant participants to determined competitors, from typical urban kids to 'ladies and gentlemen,' on their way to try to compete in the final citywide competition."[6] The film was very successful, and has since served as the inspiration for *Take the Lead*, a feature film starring Antonio Banderas. The fortuitous timing of the documentary's release caused it to factor as a recurrent topic in my discussions with informants, many of whom saw and loved the film because it resonated with their own common-sense belief that ballroom dance is a transformative and ennobling activity. In a highly emotional interview from the film, Allison Sheniak, an elementary school teacher at P.S. 150 (one of the participating schools), articulates one of the central themes of the documentary:

> I really would love not to be involved in this process [selecting team members to represent the school in the ballroom dance competition quarterfinals] because they're all my kids and just . . . I don't want to choose favorites. I don't want to pick

> one over the other because I don't want to hurt anyone. I wish all the kids could just pair up and compete in ballroom dancing. That would be the best way. I see them turning into, [long pause] I'm going to cry, [long pause, and then continues while crying] I see them turning into these ladies and gentlemen," . . . [breaks down in tears and ends the interview].

The film suggests that the children have two options; either fall victim to the vice and crime on the streets of New York or opt for ballroom dance, which provides a way out. Most choose the ballroom, and the uplifting final scenes are meant to convince us that, in fact, they have been saved through ballroom dance. My informants liked the film, in large part because they too believed that ballroom dancing was inherently good and that it contained the promise of salvation and transformation for at-risk children as well as the general public. The belief that ballroom dancing has the power to turn brutes into gentlemen is not a recent phenomenon. Throughout the history of the dance industry, dance masters have encouraged parents to enroll their children in dance classes for its "civilizing" benefits, and in particular for its ability to train young people in the proper conventions of upper-class, heterosexual socializing (Bosse 2004; Cook 1998; Malnig 1992; Tomko 1999; Wagner 1997).

Ladies and gentlemen, princesses and princes, such idealized gendered constructs are powerful mechanisms with which ballroomers score their own dancing. Such performance informs life off of the dance floor and inscribes dancers' beliefs in their own potential onto their body and their self-imaginary. Ethnomusicologist Jane Sugarman makes a similar point in her analysis of Albanian wedding singers:

> It is an experience that endures through the vagaries of daily life to serve as a point of reference, an index to Prespa femaleness and maleness. In their everyday lives they are not held to every detail of what they experience through such stylized behavior, since what they set forth through their [performance] is an imaginatively constructed ideal. But they can measure their behavior against that ideal and decide to what degree they wish to diverge from the community standards that they, through their performances, help to define (1989, 208).

These norms for heterosexual socializing rely on gendered identities, constructs that ballroom dancers both corroborate and contradict with their lives on and off the dance floor.

Whether performed by an upper-class divorcée in an affluent ballroom studio or by urban children in their school gymnasium, ballroom dance is experienced and interpreted by students and teachers alike as a transformative act that structures and is structured by deep cultural archetypes of gendered identity. Becoming beautiful through ballroom dance is, to a significant degree, about becoming gendered. The educated elites I worked with understood the arbitrary and yet powerful nature of gender in contemporary American social life from the abstract theoretical perspective of the academy as well as through the brute reality of their everyday experiences. For these individuals, and especially for women who have transgressed traditional female roles by having professional careers, performing gender in the most idealized sense within the isolated contexts of the ballroom helps settle the shifting sands. While in their everyday world they may be smart and successful, in the ballroom they become beautiful women, full and idealized gendered social beings. In learning about lead and follow, reciprocity and connection, gender is performed according to a very specific set of codes and conventions that govern bodily movements and bodily responses. In training one's body to "suggest" (lead) a move and/or to respond to a suggestion (follow), dancers critically engage gendered ideas of dominance and submission, invitation and answer in order to construct and reconstruct themselves as gendered subjects.

Mastering the art of partnership—the push and pull of accommodating another and of sharing yourself in movement and music—is central to the kind of "beautification" that occurs on the dance floor. Connection is one of the genre's most affective aspects and the distinguishing factor that separates it from other kinds of dance. It is powerful because it is suggestive of the potential for normative heterosexual connection and for one's own ability to be felt and to be known by another person. This lies at the heart of what becoming beautiful is about—becoming connected, known, received, accepted, and embraced.

4

Performing Race, Remaking Whiteness

I was milling about the lobby of the Regent Ballroom and Banquet Center in Savoy, Illinois, chatting with a group of ballroom dancers who were preparing for their first salsa formation dance team rehearsal. One dancer in particular, Ethan, was very eager to get started. He was pacing the floor, snapping his fingers nervously, and practicing the basic salsa moves he already knew, accompanied by music he hummed to himself. Among salsa dancers Ethan was a notoriously mediocre dancer who received unenthusiastic responses to his invitations to salsa dance. He was, however, a proficient ballroom dancer, and I asked him why he was so anxious to learn salsa, a genre that seemed particularly difficult for him, when he already possessed a high degree of skill in so many other dances. "I want to get ethnic!" he quickly responded, "I'm tired of being white."

Although few stated the issue in such bald terms, Ethan's characterization of his own dance experiences, highlighting dance's potential to transform one's sense of one's own racial identity, was not uncommon. Many of the ballroom dancers I worked with spoke of race metaphorically and connected their "true" racial identity to their ability (or lack thereof) to perform various types of dance genres. In particular, ballroom dancers racialized the broad generic subdivisions of "Standard" and "Latin," the two fundamental categories of ballroom dance. This chapter explores the implications of their remarks regarding the Standard and Latin categories and the racial stereotypes encoded within them.

Scholarship on whiteness has suggested that status of whiteness as a tacit, taken-for-granted category is inherently unstable (Dyer 1997; Frankenburg 1997; Levine-Rasky 2002, Roediger 1990). The diffuse and paradoxical meaning of whiteness, its ability to represent both a specific subject (the white "race") and a universal subject (the human race), renders the concept unstable, even as it infuses it with symbolic power. Its instability requires that it always be maintained, that the concept is always in the process of being made and unmade. Similarly, anthropologist Arjun Appadurai has observed, "Minorities in many parts of the world are as artificial as the majorities they are seen to threaten: 'whites' in the United States, Hindus in India, Englishmen in Great Britain, all are examples of how the political and administrative designation of some groups as 'minorities' . . . helps to pull majorities together under labels with short lives but long histories." Groups such as whites and Hispanics, he continues, "are as often made as they are born" (1993, 800). However, research that examines how whiteness is made, how it is performed in daily life, and how white dominance is rationalized, legitimized, and maintained is scant. In its exploration of the ways in which whiteness was made, and perhaps sometimes unmade, through the performance of ballroom dance, this chapter contributes to this literature and seeks to understand the ways in which the unstable status of whiteness as doxa (that is, as an unmarked category and as an unreflected-upon set of ideological constructions) is maintained through expressive practice.

Whiteness is an invention, a social construct that is independent from biological difference and skin color, even though it uses ideas about them. Dancers at the Regent Ballroom generally treated class as coterminous with race, and thus the whiteness presented in this case study is implicitly embedded in particular, class-based notions of who whites and racialized others are (or should be).

Like all racialized thinking, whiteness is relational and dialectical and includes a range of processes of inclusion and exclusion. Historically, the colonial encounter fostered the notion of a marked, visible, and racialized "other" as it simultaneously gave whiteness both its prominence and invisibility—its normativity and unmarkedness.[1] Thus, the "unmarked self" and the "racialized other" have become profoundly entwined in American cultural narratives and tacit codes of interaction and identification.

These two conceptual categories, unmarked self and racialized other, have informed the development of ballroom dance and serve to structure performance for the midwestern American dancers with whom I worked. Through the genre subclassifications of "Standard" and "Latin," whiteness was made universal and normative, rational and beautiful, while the racial other was made particular and exotic, physical and sexual. Ultimately, both are manifestations of whiteness, mirrored reflections of one another that help to define whiteness both by making invisible what it is and explicitly pronouncing what it is not. Thus, the generic subdivisions of ballroom dance genres of Standard and Latin provide an important case study about how whiteness has been encoded in American expressive forms.

Racialized categories like whiteness are constructed through performance, are embedded within the structural properties of ballroom dance, and conceptually, musically, and kinesthetically internalized through performance. My attention to different realms—movement, music, language, and physical deportment and costume—is meant to underscore the importance of redundancy across social domains for affirming and naturalizing racialized thinking. Furthermore, the sheer multiplicity of signs in ballroom dance that reference race is the means by which the concept itself is constructed and deconstructed through performance. As Phyllis Gorfain writes in her analysis of wordplay and body puns in Hamlet, "[P]lay with words deconstructs the polyvalency and mortality of symbols, which possess both an abstract level of signification and a material dimension of being. Physical symbols locate ideas in a naturalized experience and simultaneously interpret experience in abstraction. Symbols make matter matter" (1993, 63). Similarly, the combination of linguistic, visual, kinesthetic, musical, and material realms simultaneously naturalizes constructs of race in the material dimension of being, abstracts such constructs through cognitive categories and symbols, and reifies them through their unreflected-upon repetition.

Standard and Latin

Within the ballroom canon the competition dances hold a special pride of place as the heart of the repertory, even for noncompetitors, and they are, in turn, subdivided into the two large divisions of Standard and Latin.[2] Through weekly practice and formalized private and classroom instruction dancers perform several genres in each of these two main categories.

Both categories structure central messages of stereotypically racialized characters—the graceful white European and the hot-blooded Latin American—

fueling the self-imaginary and performance experiences of everyday dancers. These archetypes of self and racialized other operate through the performance codes defining each category and are embodied through performance. Through this very basic categorization of genres, dancers construct whiteness both implicitly and explicitly. The standard category cultivates whiteness through the celebration of a romanticized construction of "Europeanness" and related ideas about classicism and sophistication. A more tacit though no less powerful construction of whiteness is engaged through the performance of Latin genres. That is to say, whiteness in many other cultural and social domains is almost always constructed in opposition to an ideological Otherness: the Standard dances are only known as such because there exists a Latin category to stand alongside. The division of ballroom dance into these two dance categories articulates the dialectical and relational aspects of whiteness and racial categories more generally.

It is important to remember that whiteness, like all racial categories, exists apart from the actual skin color of any particular individual. One need not be white to perform whiteness, and, in fact, my employment of the concept suggests that the small number of racial minorities at the Regent—primarily Asian and Asian American dancers, as well as the two African American dancers and occasional Latin American participants—were also performing whiteness through their participation in the genre while simultaneously they might also have been performing other aspects of their identity, racial and otherwise (Uba 2007).[3]

Performing the Standard Dances

The Standard genres were most often characterized by my informants as "elegant," "classic," and "beautiful." They were discussed as manifestations of a shared past, dances from "our grandparents' generation," or, as one dancer put it, "when men were men and women were women." Stylistically speaking, they are traveling dances, meaning that the couple travels counterclockwise around the dance floor in closed position. Part of the power of the Standard dances is the size of the movement, the length of the stride, the scale of posture, and the perpetual forward, floating momentum, called body flight. The closed position for these dances requires an elongated spine, locked torso, and expanded frame. Assuming this position is a theatrical gesture, but it is also a kind of political one, commanding space and attention as one traverses the entire floor.

Women Standard dancers performed in pastel or sherbet-colored ball gowns, tight in the bodice with a fuller, flowing skirt and adorned with feathers, rhine-

Figure 2: Ballroom dance competitors. Standard category. Photograph by Carson Zullinger. Courtesy of Carson Zullinger.

Figure 3: Ballroom dance competitors. Standard category. Photograph by Carson Zullinger. Courtesy of Carson Zullinger.

stones, or jewels. The hair is almost always swept high on the head in a French twist or bun and is generally dyed to platinum blonde if possible. Makeup, like hair color, tends to gravitate toward extremes of either powdery, porcelain white (if coupled with dark hair) or deep, bronze tan (if coupled with blonde). Men perform in traditional black tuxedoes with tails (see figures 2 and 3).[4]

Orchestral accompaniment predominates in the Standard genres, especially those at the top of the canon. Further down the Standard hierarchy, in the foxtrot and quickstep genres, one is more likely to find solo or ensemble vocals (especially Frank Sinatra), a greater variety of instrumental accompaniments, and the frequent use of arrangements of once popular songs from Tin Pan Alley, Broadway, or later radio and dance band hits. Many of the compositions for this category predate the 1960s or emulate these earlier styles. While certain classical composers have written Viennese waltzes that are occasionally used for ballroom dance, most of the music that accompanies these dance genres is not "classical" in the sense used by musicologists. It was, however, often described as "classical" by my informants. Dancers often stated that the sophisticated nature of the classical music was one of the most appealing aspects of ballroom dancing—and especially the Standard genres. Generally, the more signifiers of European art music found in the music associated with a genre—string orchestras, symmetrical periodicity and form, melody-dominated textures, and so forth—the more prestigious a position the genre holds in the canon.

Performing the Latin Dances

The Latin genres were most frequently characterized as "sexy," "hot," and "fun" by the dancers with whom I worked. All genres in the Latin category are spot dances, meaning the couple does not travel around but remains (basically) fixed in one spot on the floor. The frame is smaller and more relaxed, with elbows held lower and close to the body; the steps are paced more quickly but smaller in stride length.[5] Ballroom Latin genres involve a technique called "Latin walks" (or "Cuban walks") that uses counterbody motion of the knee, hip, and ribcage for each step taken and are said to provide the characteristic torso movement for which these genres are admired.

Women competitors in the Latin division wear very tightly fitted rhinestone or jewel-studded dresses that are generally shorter and designed with slits and cutouts to reveal (or appear to reveal) more skin. Dresses in a variety of vibrant colors—black, jewel, or neon tones—adorned with metallic sequins are paired with open-toe shoes with strappy heels. Hairstyles generally mimic a combination of the flamenco dancer and gypsy stereotypes with jet black, glossy hair combed close to the head and sculpted with waves and curls near the nape and cheekbones. Men, too, sport glossy, dark hair, styled long and straight and often secured in a ponytail at the nape of the neck. Forsaking the tuxedo, men in the Latin division typically perform in a blousy, sateen shirt often left open to the torso, black slacks, and a slightly higher heeled shoe (called Latin heels). Both men and women use dark eye makeup and darken their skin tone (see figures 4 and 5).[6] While it is not typical for social ballroom dances to adorn themselves in this way, I do wonder about the degree to which such signifiers may factor in the self-imaginary of social dancers, regardless of their outward appearance.

In the Latin category, musical accompaniment also involves string orchestras, especially for rhumba and bolero. More prevalent, however, are jazz and dance bands featuring brass instruments, piano, a rhythm section with extensive hand percussion, and vocalists. While the Latin genres make use of instrumental compositions created expressly for ballroom dancing, radio hits, such as Carlos Santana's hit "Smooth" and ballroom arrangements of popular

Figure 4: Ballroom dance competitors. Latin category. Photograph by Carson Zullinger. Courtesy of Carson Zullinger.

Figure 5: Ballroom dance competitors. Latin Category. Photograph by Carson Zullinger. Courtesy of Carson Zullinger.

songs, were more fashionable. The use of voices and popular song increases as one moves further down the hierarchy. The issue is made more complex by the possibility of Spanish-language lyrics, which, depending on other aspects of the arrangement, can add an air of cosmopolitan sophistication, especially to the slower rhumba. "Hearing" and dancing correctly in time with the complex rhythmic component of some Latin music was cited as one of the most challenging aspects of the Latin dance genres (especially the cha cha). In fact, for many dancers I worked with, the rhythmic counterpoint served as the sonic signifier of the physical energy—perceived to be more raw than refined—of Latin dancing more generally.[7]

Turning now to what my informants had to say about these classifications, I draw from survey and interview responses of ballroom dancers at the Regent. When asked to name her favorite dance, Rita, one of the few African American ballroom dancers to attend the Regent regularly, responded:

> My favorite ballroom dances are samba and waltz. I adore samba because of the music. It made me want to jump up and move long before I learned how to do

> the dance; I just totally "get" samba on some elemental level—perhaps I was born in Brazil in another life. My enjoyment of the waltz, on the other hand, is more about the way I feel when I do it. It's an elegant dance that allows even basically klutzy people to feel like real dancers.

This quote contains elements that are representative of a number of larger trends I observed throughout my fieldwork. First, Rita opted to name one favorite dance in the Standard division (waltz) and another from the Latin (samba). Her compulsion to name not one dance but two, one each in the subcategories of Standard and Latin, was common among the dancers with whom I worked. Many dancers did this, or inquired if that was, in fact, what I actually meant to ask.

This hierarchical structure of genres is understood and accepted by all who participated in ballroom dance at my fieldsite and is used both as a key pedagogical tool and as the organizing principle for local, regional, national, and international competitions. Thus, at all levels of participation, from beginners to professionals, these categories operated to inform and structure dance experiences. In fact, I have never met a dancer, regardless of his or her own racial identification, for whom these categories were anything but an assumed, natural, or common-sense way to understand the variety of dances performed. All the dancers I knew accepted this hierarchy of genres and participated in its maintenance.

David built his entire dance pedagogy on these two categories, highlighting their differences while emphasizing their complementarity. An examination of his curriculum (see figure 6) reveals that in each course he combined an equal mixture of Standard and Latin genres. Similarly, he also arranged the Friday evening dances to include an equal measure of each category, paired in sets, as is demonstrated on the dance card for a Friday night dance (see figure 7), which contains fourteen Standard dances, fifteen Latin dances, six Nightclub, and one polka. There is a pedagogical reason for doing so. Each category is composed of a set of stylistic features, and each requires a different technique. A well-rounded dancer, Lin argued, dances both to develop these two sets of skills.

Thus, from the very early days of learning the genre through to the highest levels of achievement, performance was structured by the notion of this duality, which was reified by its redundant and doxic quality in every dance occasion. This became clear when I surveyed David's students about their favorite ballroom dance. As did Rita, most of them felt obliged to speak to both categories, articulating their awareness of the importance and complementarity of both. For instance, Karyn, a white, middle-aged dancer said this:

> I like the modern dances. I like their "flow" and the way they move and fill space. I like the way they project "outward." Very elegant, classic. I do like Latin [dances],

1st Course Waltz Foxtrot Rumba Swing			
2nd Course Waltz Foxtrot Rumba Swing Cha Cha			
3rd Course A Waltz Rumba Samba East Coast Swing Triple Swing	3rd Course B Foxtrot Cha cha Tango Quickstep (Polka)		
4th Course A Waltz Rumba Merengue	4th Course B Bolero Samba Triple Swing	4th Course C Tango Cha cha East Coast Swing Viennese Waltz	4th Course D Foxtrot Mambo Quickstep
5th Course A Waltz Rumba Merengue	5th Course B Bolero Samba Triple Swing	5th Course C Tango Cha cha East Coast Swing Viennese Waltz	5th Course D Foxtrot Mambo Quickstep
6th Course A Waltz Rumba Merengue	6th Course B Bolero Samba Triple Swing	6th Course C Tango Cha cha East Coast Swing Viennese Waltz	6th Course D Foxtrot Mambo Quickstep
7th Course A Waltz Rumba Merengue	7th Course B Bolero Samba Triple Swing	7th Course C Tango Cha cha East Coast Swing	7th Course D Foxtrot Mambo Quickstep
8th Course A Waltz Cha cha Triple Swing	8th Course B Foxtrot Mambo Tango	8th Course C Quickstep Samba Rumba	
Advanced A Waltz Cha cha	Advanced B Samba Foxtrot		
Hustle I	Hustle II	Hustle III	
2-Step I	2-Step II	2-Step III	
West Coast Swing I	West Coast Swing II		
Salsa I	Salsa II	Salsa III	
Argentine Tango 1A Argentine Tango	Argentine Tango 1B Milonga, Vals Vals		

Figure 6: Regent curriculum of courses and course content. Courses numbered by level of difficulty. In 1996 the polka was a standard offering in 3rd Course B, but it was gradually eliminated from course offerings altogether and polkas are rarely played during Tuesday and Friday night dances.

> but they require more "compactness" in their movement. And the focus/projection is more toward your partner, which I find less comfortable to do properly. Maybe my comfort level would change if I danced with a "significant other."

Even though Karyn preferred the modern dances for their classic elegance, she felt obliged to comment on the Latin dances, communicating her awareness that the two categories were complementary and that she knew something about the Latin technique, even if she found them less comfortable to execute properly.

#1 Waltz Rumba	#8 2- Step Hustle	#15 2-Step Hustle
#2 Swing Foxtrot	#9 Waltz (2) Rumba	#16 Foxtrot Rumba
#3 Cha Cha Rumba	#10 Foxtrot Samba	#17 Quickstep (2) Triple Swing
#4 Swing Quickstep (2)	#11 Swing Cha Cha	#18 Tango Cha Cha
#5 Waltz (2) Cha Cha	#12 Break Time	#19 Swing Waltz (2)
#6 Foxtrot Triple Swing	#13 Mixer Waltz (2)	
#7 Rumba Tango	#14 Swing Polka	Goodnight N 11/5/99

Tango Demo
Argentine Tango demonstration will be performed next Friday by Alberto Paz and Valorie Hart from California.

Dance Competition
The Dancing Illini competition is on Saturday, November 6 from 9:00a-8:00p at the Illini Student Union-rooms A, B, and C. You can purchase tickets at the door.

New Year's Eve Reservation
Bring in the new year with all your friends at the Regent. Enjoy: Dinner Buffet, Open Bar, Party Favors, Champagne Toast and MUCH, MUCH MORE! Seating is limited. Reserve your place tonight. $75.00 per person

New Nightclub Classes
Salsa I and Westcoast Swing I will be offered in January. Both classes will be taught in a split room, space is limited. Pre-Enroll tonight!

Next Friday
Advanced Dance
Hot Chocolate at the break

If Your Birthday Or Anniversary Is Within Four Days Of Tonight.Let Us Help You Celebrate With A Bottle Of Champagne Or A Pitcher Of Soft Drink. Do Let Us Know Before The Break.

Figure 7: Regent dance card for Friday night dance, November 5, 1999.

A second important idea expressed in Rita's statement is the notion that the samba was something one can "get" without formal training. The suggestion that samba moved Rita in an immediately physical way, making her want to jump up and move long before she learned the dance, grounded her ability to perform it in some sort of biological, and hence, natural (or, to use her word, "elemental") experience. Her characterization of the samba as "elemental," something that one can simply "get" without formal training, is telling. In seeking an explanation for why this may be so, she suggests that perhaps she was "born in Brazil in another life," positing a metaphorical, if not literal, biological and ancestral connection to the region, thus situating her performance of the samba within the discourse of race.

The reference to some sort of metaphorical Latin "blood" or "soul" was overwhelming in my work, while I never once heard a similar construction used to justify the performance of the Standard genres (see Bosse 1999, 2004, 2007; Lausevic 1998, 2007; Waters 1990). Deborah Kapchan's analysis of the Moroccan art of henna body painting provides an interesting vantage point from which to understand ballroom dancers' attempts to naturalize their performances of Latin dance. Comparing henna to more permanent forms of body art, she states: "There is a definite dialogue between the ephemeral art of henna and its indelible counterpart, tattoo. Even though henna is a transient art, its vocabulary strains toward images of permanency" (1993, 26). So, too, does the symbolic vocabulary of Latin dance performance strain toward images of permanency as a naturalized, "primal," or "elemental" condition of existence. The practice of darkening skin tones, the use of hair color, and the development of new physical habits that become a part of one's everyday physical vocabulary blur the boundaries between temporary performance or theatrical costume and everyday life and contribute to the feeling that one has discovered his or her own exotic blood.

The Latin genres were often associated with sexuality and sexual relationships, thus Karyn's belief that were she to dance these with a "significant other," presumably someone with whom she was physically intimate, her performance might have been improved. Even the direct eye contact of these genres incited feelings of greater intimacy among dancers of Latin genres. In this context, it is important to clarify that intimacy itself is a constructed notion of relationships and has no universal or objective standard. Among the dancers I worked with, intimacy was generally measured by the degree to which individuals felt embarrassed, vulnerable, or exposed within their partnership.

While most dancers suggested the Latin dances were more intimate, a small number admitted embarrassment when dancing the Standard genres with certain partners. While they were not strongly associated with sexuality, the advanced-level performance of Standard genres mandated physical contact from the thigh to the ribcage, with the legs moving between those of one's partner. Several dancers joked nervously about this level of proximity. For example, while leaving the dance floor after a waltz, Louise, a single, white female, shuddered, "Ugh, I'm so glad that dance is over. It creeped me out to feel his thing-y [euphemism for penis]." Interestingly, very few dancers interpreted these feelings of embarrassment, the degree of physical contact, or the close proximity of the genitalia and the lower torsos of the dancers characteristic of the Standard genres as being a signifier of the genre's intimacy.

In addition to the words "sexy," "hot," and "fun," another word frequently associated with the Latin dances was "sensual." Relevant here is dance scholar Jane Desmond's suggestion that the term references a "sophisticated" kind of sexuality preferred among white, upper-class audiences (1997, 40–43)—a sexuality that is highly codified and stylized. For instance, Tilly, who identified as Caucasian, stated that her favorite dance was the rumba: "It provides me a chance to express my sensuality while being very graceful. I enjoy the interactions with my partner—we can have eye contact while dancing. It is not as stylized as the waltz." In fact, the Latin genres were often considered an opportunity to explore and express one's own sexuality within the conventions of polite society. This is coded in Tilly's quote by the desire to be sensual while also being graceful. Although occasionally interpreted this way by outsiders, the performance of Latin genres were not intended to lampoon Latin Americans. Rather, their performance represents an attempt to develop one's own sense of self as a sexual or sensual being, something many dancers admitted to feeling insecure about.

Whether rooted in sexuality or bloodlines, dancers discussed the Latin genres as being more explicitly embodied, as more natural, biological, "elemental," or, as another stated it, "primal." As Irene, a white dancer trained in ballet, stated, she liked the Latin dances because they were more "organic" than the other genres she already knew and said that the "undulating waves" of the music were more "natural" and better matched her body. As another dancer more baldly noted, "[Modern] is a dance of rules for the brain; Latin is a dance without rules for the body."

Returning once again to Rita's remarks about her favorite Standard dance, the waltz: "My enjoyment of the waltz, on the other hand, is more about the way I feel when I do it. It's an elegant dance that allows even basically klutzy people to feel like real dancers." Description of the Standard dances, and particularly the waltz as elegant, was ubiquitous at my fieldsite. Indeed, the waltz was once described to me by a competitor as the "crown jewel of ballroom dance." Other common descriptors were "classic" and "beautiful"; "graceful" was also used frequently, and women dancers testified that they liked to dance the Standard genres because doing so made them feel more graceful and beautiful. Rita suggested that what she liked about the waltz was its ability to elevate her own dancing, that she was made to feel elegant rather than klutzy, to feel as if she were a more competent dancer than she actually believed herself to be. In fact, during the course of my fieldwork, several women reiterated this point precisely. When I asked Caucasian dancer Bridget about her favorite genre, she replied, "[I have] just one. Waltz. I feel beautiful when I dance it." The floating quality of the genre was cited again and again as one of the salient characteristics of the dance. Ruth, a white American, said she loved the waltz "because it is graceful and flowing." Robby said he "loved to float across the floor to the rise and fall of each note." Similarly, Toby, of Vietnamese descent, liked the waltz for its "grace and feeling of floating movement." Embedded in this discourse lies a double metaphor. Dancing the Standard genres, one feels as if he or she is floating just above the floor. I have felt this feeling myself when dancing the Standard genres with the right partner. But in these testimonies we hear of a different kind of elevation as well.

Through the performance of the Standard dances, one can be "elevated" from an awkward and average-looking person to a graceful and beautiful dancer. It is important to highlight here that the Standard dances were deeply encoded to symbolize whiteness, dominant culture, and European conventions. When dancers suggest that these dances are beautiful, they are participating in the maintenance of whiteness by connecting the concept of beauty to indicators of whiteness. References to such concepts are not at all neutral or relative but lie instead at the heart of how race is constructed.

While performing the Standard genres may have felt good, however, one did not learn them "by feel" but through disciplined practice. I can recall only one dancer who referred to any of the Standard dances as feeling natural, or as having taken to the dances naturally, as was common with the Latin genres. Grace, elegance, and sophistication, all hallmarks of the Standard genres, were only achievable through controlled movement. When I was working on the foxtrot in private lessons with David, he stated it this way: "People might think the foxtrot is easy, but it is, in fact, one of the hardest to do. Sure you can step through the steps and the rhythm isn't complicated. But the subtle timing, the pushing forward with the feet—all of it has to look relaxed and effortless, but it is hard work."[8]

Nightclub or "Street" Dances

This chapter focuses on the heart of the ballroom repertory, the competition dances of Standard and Latin. I would like to digress here to discuss a third category employed at the Regent, the Nightclub genres, or what were colloquially referred to as "street" dances. In general, the "street" dances performed at the Regent were all popularized post-1960, were closely connected with the expressive culture of the African diaspora, and existed at the margins of codified ballroom practice. Not part of official competitive practice, the performance of the Nightclub genres is highly variable from one site to the next. There is no official ballroom curriculum for these genres. Some studios do not offer them at all; others offer some of them only as a "break" from the more serious lessons. The Regent offered the hustle, West Coast swing, mambo, salsa, merengue, and Nightclub two-step.

At the Regent, the Nightclub dances were segregated from the core ballroom courses. They were taught in their own classes apart from the conventional ballroom curriculum, and, as can be seen on the dance card, were paired to form their own sets on Friday night dances. At the Regent, various "street" dances fell in and out of fashion, in part according to the whims of David and what he was interested in teaching. For some time, salsa was the most popular "street" dance. Salsa dance studios sprang up across the region and salsa dance events took place three to six times per week (see also Bosse 2004, 2008a, 2013b, 2013c). The merengue enjoyed a brief surge of popularity because of its close association with salsa, and the same is true for bachata as well, although to a lesser degree. Nightclub two-step, a slow dance usually danced to rhythm and blues or soul music was a regular favorite among most dancers, while the hustle remained a cult favorite for a few stalwart fans.

During my last visit to the region, David was ramping up his instruction of West Coast swing, in part because of lobbying from his students but also because he thought it the most flexible for use in nonballroom dance contexts. He liked the potential for virtuosity, and he thought the music was more interesting. Any dance that emerges in popular culture may be granted a place in the Nightclub category, depending on whether or not dancers are interested in performing it in the context of the ballroom. For instance, the rueda (a collective, round-dance variant of salsa) enjoyed a brief period of popularity at the Regent. It was included in the Nightclub sets and breaks during the Friday night dances before falling out of favor about nine months later. Other ballroom dance studios may not offer any Nightclub dances, or they may offer some but not others, as per the interests of the teachers and the clientele.

The Nightclub category serves as a repository for any genre that might be enjoyable to perform or that is perceived to possess the potential to be included in the more formalized ballroom repertory with some modification. They were generally perceived to be less sophisticated than their core ballroom counterparts. As Sophia, a highly accomplished competitive dancer complained, "I don't know what the big deal is. All these salsa dancers are doing is the same move over and over with no discipline. It's chaos. I'm sorry, but it's on the verge of vertical sex!" While many ballroom dancers enjoyed dancing salsa and would have taken issue with Sophia's characterization, they would have been sympathetic with the underlying assumption that salsa is less sophisticated than the conventional ballroom genres. In fact, the other dancers present when Sophia made her claim argued with her that with some "attention," salsa had the potential to be another great dance in the lineage that included rumba and cha cha. This sentiment echoes Arthur Murray's sentiment about the rumba, made more than fifty years earlier: "The rumba, which originated in Cuba, is unique among ballroom dances. The music has a seductive, primitive charm, and yet, when correctly danced, the Rumba is as smooth as the Fox Trot, as decorous as the Waltz" (1954, 110).

Placed alongside the Standard and Latin dance categories, the "street" dances provide a foil that reveals what "sophistication" means, and in particular, the racial and class-based prejudices that inform it. As the Latin category provided an opportunity to perform a particular kind of racialized exoticism that was aligned with the genre's middle-class concepts of sophistication, the "street" category served as the catchall for the racialized genres that were not closely aligned with the ballroom dancers' class-based sensibilities. Not coincidentally, many of these genres remained stylistically closer to their original versions than their counterparts in the Latin and Standard categories, which have undergone significant stylistic modification and codification.

Rather than an expressly racialized category like the Latins, the genres in this category are identified by place. In particular, they are located in the metaphorical "street," where dancing is less codified and perceived to be less refined. Locating these genres in "the street" identifies them as both racialized and classified. Just as the "Modern" category signifies urbane (and white) "Europeanness" by situating it temporally in the now (and the future, as the term "modern" often implies), the "street" dances signify blackness by situating them in the danger of the "urban jungle."

Perhaps one of the remarkable aspects of these various canonical discourses and lexicons is the degree to which they silence contribution of African America and the African diaspora both in terms of general stylistic influence and the contribution of particular genres. While only occasionally noted in common parlance, ballroom owes a great debt to African American and Afro-Caribbean performance, both in terms of the movement as well as the musical styles that informed the dancing. Most notable is the swing complex, which originated in African American communities before dance masters codified it for a broader audience in the 1930s. Samba and rumba, originally from Afro-Caribbean communities (Brazil and Cuba, respectively), also underwent significant modifications at the hands of dance masters in the first half of the twentieth century. Furthermore, African American performance influenced the development of many other ballroom genres, including the cha cha, foxtrot, quickstep, hustle, mambo, salsa, merengue, bachata, and West Coast swing. This does not even begin to address the influence of a range of dances that are no longer performed, such as the rag and animal dances, one-step, and so forth. As Brenda Dixon-Stowell notes, "The history of black popular dance is also the history of white popular dance. . . . The black influence in America, always a potent force in shaping the New World Aesthetic, became increasingly part of white American mainstream culture" (1988, 352). Over the past century, ballroom dance has absorbed many elements from African American performance into its movement vocabulary, so that all the dances that fall under the "ballroom umbrella" have been stylistically touched by those elements. Through the legacy of black performance, American couple-dance styles have experienced what Cornel West has called the "Afro-Americanization" of the Western body (1993, 84).

Many of my informants were cognizant of the fact that Black Americans were influential in social dance history and certain ballroom genres in particular, but I often found it remarkable how little this aspect of ballroom history was discussed, especially compared with the frequent and obvious remarks on the contributions of Latin America. To some degree, the mechanism by which genres are categorized into Standard, Latin, and Nightclub divisions, irrespective of their geographic or cultural origins, allows the influence of black America to be obscured, if not silenced altogether (Trouillot 1995). Just as the Latin category was not about the actual lived experiences of Latinos but was instead a figurative notion of "Latinness" as constructed by whites, likewise the experiences of black Americans, the African Americans and Afro-Caribbeans whose influence informs contemporary ballroom performance, are also silenced in the generic discourse and practice of ballroom dance. The stylistic influence of black American dance is undeniable, but through the lexicon of the genre, contemporary performers are able to avoid confronting the contributions of black Americans and the legacy of racism that has denied black Americans their place in ballroom dance's history and its future.

As is evident in the response to Sophia's comment above, the category of "street" dances has served as the gateway for acceptance into the core codified ballroom repertory. As new dances have emerged in popular culture and come to the attention of ballroom dancers, dance masters have placed themselves in the position of cultural translators capable of modifying the popular genre for performance in the ballroom. In fact, many genres underwent a stylistic transformation from a "street" or Nightclub variant that was then transformed by dance professionals into a style considered more appropriate for polite society, a role they have cast themselves in for more than a hundred years (Bosse 1999, 2008a; Cook 1998; Malnig 1992; Wagner 1997).

Ballroom history is rife with examples of dance masters cultivating fear of Latin American and African American dances in order to promote their own modified versions as being more "safe" for white consumption. In the 1930s, proponents of the rumba pointed to the success of its predecessor, the tango, as an exemplar for the potential beauty that the Latin American genres could yield if performed properly—that is, according to the steps created and taught by dance masters. During the 1930s, as the swing and rumba were both competing for mainstream attention, dance masters proposed to white parents that they should enroll their children in ballroom rumba lessons taught by dance masters rather than let their children fall prey to the wild abandon of the (African American) swing, which at that time had not yet been modified for white performance. Rumba, as it was performed in the ballroom, was portrayed as exotic enough to entice white American youth without the risks of the "too exotic" swing.

The academic treatment of this and similar phenomena has often employed the notions of "whitewashing" or "domestication," as if these concepts are clearly articulated theoretical frameworks that have been tested by the rigors of intellectual inquiry. While I do not take issue with the evocation of race and class that are implied in the terminology, these ideological constructs mask the complexities of the processes to which they are attributed and gloss over a complicated reality that begs more detailed study (Bosse 2004, 2008a).

Essentialism and the Performance of Race

As dance scholar Jane Desmond suggests, "Dance, as a discourse of the body, may in fact be especially vulnerable to interpretations in terms of essentialized identities associated with biological difference. These identities include race and gender and the sexualized associations attached to bodies marked in these terms" (1997, 36–37). The fact that dancing is a bodily discourse only enhances the perception of these sexual characteristics as "true." The pleasure aspect of social dancing often obscures our awareness of it as a symbolic system, so that dances are often seen as "authentic" unmediated expressions and are taken as evidence of a racial character.

This certainly rings true for the Latin genres and their perception at the Regent. The stylistic qualities of the dances—the hip action, eye contact, and emphasis on syncopated rhythm—were perceived as sexual and as evidence of the sexual nature of Latin Americans more generally. An ability to perform these genres was rooted in biological difference, race, and ancestry—even when these justifications depended on manufactured metaphors of a "Latin soul." It is important to remember, however, that the performance of ballroom Latin genres does not really tell us about Latin Americans. Rather, it speaks volumes about white America and the ways public expression of white sexuality and rhythmic engagement is encoded in racialized terms.

Due to its tacit nature, it is more difficult to tackle the issues of how whiteness was signified in the performance of Standard genres. Whiteness was frequently submerged and alternatively coded as a set of universal aesthetic values (grace, beauty, and elegance) even though the signifiers of these values (the blonde hair, ball gowns and tuxedoes, and use of string orchestras labeled "classical music") were tacitly embedded in white, upper-class notions of beauty.

To seek this kind of aesthetic experience, the dancers say it is one's discipline that must be developed, and thus it was not necessary to justify one's ability to perform the Standard dances in any kind of natural tendency or racial or ethnic heritage, literal or otherwise. This was true even for the small number of black, Latino/Latina, or Asian dancers. As the universal standard for all couple dancing, it was considered entirely appropriate for people of all races and ethnic backgrounds to desire to perform them well. I never heard an Asian dancer legitimate her performance of the waltz in a metaphorical European blood; no one ever claimed to have been born in Germany in another life.[9]

In her study of white Americans and ethnicity, sociologist Mary Waters concludes that although ethnicity among the white middle class is not perceived to have direct relevance or ramifications on their everyday lives (in other words, it does not affect where they live or what type of job they have), it is believed to be the source of personality traits. For example, if one is uptight or emotionally demonstrative, if one speaks with large hand gestures or is particularly seductive, these are perceived to be qualities attributed to one's ethnicity. She also suggests that claiming some degree of ethnicity "fulfills [a] particularly American need to be 'from somewhere'" (1990, 150). The "American" need is not only to have a sense of ancestral history and to be part of a larger social collective but also to feel simultaneously unique, a result of the importance of "individuality" in the American psyche. American democracy and the demise of aristocracy, the distinctly American celebration of individualism, and technological advancements significantly altered the ways European Americans have connected to their community and family, resulting in a void left by the demise of close familial ties (nuclear and extended) and community associations. Technological advancements such as the automobile, air conditioning, telephone, and the Internet, as well as changes in residential architecture and civil planning (suburbs), Waters points out, can be understood as contributing to a greater separation of individuals one from another, serving to weaken community ties (145–50).

Waters argues that to redress this situation, her respondents—white, middle-class Americans—selectively chose to celebrate certain aspects of their ethnicity. She calls this selective, explicit cultivation of certain aspects of ethnic identity "symbolic ethnicity," a concept originally developed by Herbert Gans (1979). For many whites, their ethnic heritage was simply too vague, complex, convoluted, or unattractive to merit celebration. This type of individual, many of whom are featured in my own ethnographic study, described themselves ambiguously or disparagingly as "Heinz 57," "mutt," "vanilla," "generic," or lacking in ethnicity at all (see also Lausevic 1998). They were aware that not only is it good to have a singular sense of ethnic identity, but also that certain ethnic identities are "better," more highly valued, than others. When asked what ethnic identity they would prefer, if they could choose from any, Waters's respondents overwhelmingly said they would choose to be part of a "living ethnicity," one that is not diluted or antiquated (like their own). In the case of third- and fourth-generation European immigrants, their ethnicity is perceived to be something other than "living"—an artificial perpetuation of outdated, inauthentic practices. Her respondents cited other groups or romanticized places—Native Americans, Gypsies, or a mythical rural homeland or ethnic ghettos—communities perceived to have stronger family ties, with rich, "thick" cultures that were not "uptight" (Waters 1990, 152).

These responses resonate strongly with those of my own case study, where Latin American culture, understood generally as a monolithic entity, was perceived as a highly desirable ethnicity (see Bosse 2008, 2013b, 2013c). Latinos were understood to have strong familial and community ties, to be physically and sexually relaxed and open without impropriety, and to possess a "living" culture, of which salsa music and dance was an integral part. Though it may have been impossible to "become" a Latino, my informants were drawn to the Latin genres as a means of acquiring the positive qualities they associated with Latin Americans. Waters (1990) suggests that for white, middle-class Americans, ethnicity is generally understood as a choice that provides some type of social pleasure—what she coins a "costless community." Whites erroneously superimpose this conception of ethnicity to others (especially racial minorities), one factor that can lead to racial misunderstandings and tensions.

We may conclude two things from Waters's study: first, that ethnic groups (or the stereotypes of certain ethnic groups) are valued relatively within larger society, and individuals measure the relative social value of their ethnic affiliation (if any) to that of other possibilities; second, that individuals who are dissatisfied with their "ethnic options" and the cultural and personality traits attributed to them (or if they feel they can make no legitimate claim to one ethnicity) turn to the cultural practices, such as music and dance, of other groups as a means of satisfying inadequacies in their own lives.

My fieldwork experiences echo Waters's research. When confronted with difference on the dance floor, whether it be through performing the cha cha in a ballroom class or sharing the dance floor with Latino dancers during a Regent salsa dance, the non-Latin dancers with whom I worked began to wrestle with ambiguous feelings about their own sensuality and sexual prowess relative to the perceptions of Latin Americans. They attributed this difference to ethnic heritage, considered their own ethnicity of relatively little value, and turned to the cultural practices of Latin Americans in hopes of finding some satisfaction. Even non-Latin, nonwhite dancers expressed that Latin American culture was relatively more prestigious (more "cool") within local social networks than their own cultural heritage from Asia, the Middle East, or the Mediterranean.

These dancers wanted to "get ethnic," to obtain the beneficial aspects they perceived to be inherent in Latin American ethnicity through the performance of Latin American genres. The performance of Latin dances helped non-Latinos remake themselves anew through the internalization of favorable aspects of Latin American ethnicity. However, this internalization, the embodiment of new physical habits understood to be more liberated, relaxed, and sexual, was not discussed as something new at all but rather as an an excavation of something that had preexisted in the self. What was described was not an internalization of a foreign other but an externalization of something within, an affirmation of the existence of an exotic self believed to be buried deep in the psyche. Beth, a European American of mixed Irish and Polish descent, said she was learning to dance salsa because it "has the spice of 'my' Latinness." Her choice to frame the word "my" in quotes characterizes the understanding that this is not a reference to any type of literal ancestral lineage but a type of metaphorical conceptualization of a "spicier," more exotic component of the self for which she has no other language. Although it was often couched in these terms, dancers did not choose to dance Latin dances because they were ultimately desirous of a Latin American ethnicity: they desired to construct for themselves an alternative sense of self that they perceived to be more "vibrant," or "alive," more physically integrated, and more sexually attractive. But there existed no language and few conceptual categories for such a construction of their own, largely unmarked identity. Latin American ethnicity, or preconceived notions of it, served as the cognitive conduit through which this type of identity could be cultivated.

I have suggested here that the performance of ballroom dance is structured by the dualistic and racialized notions of a rational self, a normalized whiteness, and an embodied, explicitly racialized other. I would reiterate, however, that in fact, whiteness is constructed by both categories. The Latin genres explicitly signify what whiteness is not, clearly demarcating its boundaries along the lines of race and sexuality. The Standard genres, while fashioned on European conventions for dress, movement, and music, are discursively deracialized, the European influence rhetorically submerged, and the genres framed simply as the normative standard for beauty.

But I also intended something more about the complementarity of these genres. The performance of both genres is required in order to become not only a well-rounded dancer, but, I would suggest, a well-rounded person as well. My informants, who at various points during my fieldwork expressed anxiety about their ethnicity and their sexuality, were interested in transforming themselves, and the decision to dance ballroom was part of this transformation. The Cartesian overtones in the above quotes—for example, "modern is a dance of rules for the brain; Latin is a dance without rules for the body"—speak to the ways in which these two categories also signify different aspects of the self. Ballroom dancers, like many Americans, subscribed to the basic premise of the Cartesian duality and perceived of themselves to be divided into two separate and distinct components—the mind and the body—powerful constructs in the shared self-imaginary of many middle- and upper-class Americans. Although it may not be the case in other arenas of American public life, ballroom dancers valued both aspects, but felt out of balance, that they were more mind than body. Part of the appeal of ballroom dance was its utility in helping to restore balance to the self, to bring mind and body together through movement to music.

Given that there exists little appropriate and positive language with which to discuss white sexuality, perhaps it should not be surprising that these dancers turned to the racial stereotype of the sexy Latin American as a means of achieving this goal of balance. In his landmark study of orientalism, Edward Said suggested something similar: "European culture gained in strength and identity by setting itself off against the Orient as a sort of surrogate and even underground self" (2003, 3). Likewise, white American ballroom dancers acquire power by juxtaposing unmarked European American practices against racialized Latin American traditions. In this context, whiteness involves learning how to inhabit the body while ever seeking its definition in the mind.

But I might also suggest a slightly different interpretation as well. While I consider ballroom dance to be a site where whiteness is maintained, one might also conclude that, at least for some dancers, there is also an attempt to unmake it as well, or at least to forge a different kind of whiteness that is itself more racialized, sexualized, and beautiful to its proponents. The juxtaposition of Standard and Latin genres afforded an opportunity for my informants to explore their own public sexuality and physicality, to perform a dance for the body without forsaking their class-based ideals of rationality, restraint, and elegance. If there is any merit to what I have suggested above, that the Latin genres really have very little to do with Latin Americans, and that they are a fabricated component of white identity modeled on the Latin American "exotic other" stereotype (itself a fabrication), then we might consider their emergence as an attempt to remake whiteness.

The potential of ballroom to reinforce existing ideas of racial identity while also creating a context in which they are open to renegotiation, play, and subtle

Interlude

Two tables are decorated with streamers and balloons in celebration of birthdays, and during the break individuals begin lighting candles and serving cake. Those birthday and anniversary celebrants claim their complimentary bottle of champagne, and the hall is filled with toasts, laughter, and quiet renditions of "Happy Birthday to You." I stop by Tony and Sarah's table to say hello and wish Tony a happy birthday. The couple began dancing eighteen months ago in preparation for their daughter's wedding, and they have enjoyed dancing ever since. They are one of the many "empty-nester" couples who arrive at the Regent hoping to reconnect now that their children are grown and gone. It seems to have worked. When they circle the floor, it is not uncommon to see them exchange gestures of affection and sweetness—an indescribable and perhaps enviable combination of young love and long-time partnership they seem to be discovering anew on the dance floor.

During the break I find myself primping in the ladies-room mirror alongside Doris. She is a divorced, independent, small-business owner who runs a seamstress shop from her home. Her remarkably mature teenage daughter watches the storefront after school while Doris mends and tailors clothes, sews beautiful slipcovers, and reupholsters furniture. In the living quarters in the back rooms of her shop, her colonial-style furniture is covered in rich colors and traditional paisley patterns. Standing in front of the mirror at the Regent, we talk about the upcoming renovations to her modest home, and her new car, a dark green Honda CR-V, which makes her smile.

We return to the ballroom together to find the mixer has begun, and we join the line of women waiting to dance. As "Dream a Little Dream" wafts over the room, Marty, a middle-aged dentist, meets me at the top of the circle, and we weave our way down the floor. His lips are pursed in concentration; he says nothing before, during, or after our dance, keeping his eyes trained on where we are headed next. I sometimes feel as if he has not even registered me here in the partnership with him. He approaches dance with an interesting intensity, as one would approach a sport, and when we complete our trip down the floor he literally sprints back into the line for the next round.

My next trip down the floor is with Don, a computer programmer who works for another ballroom dancer. He is gentle, unassuming, and wears a perpetual smile. He has been dancing for two years and is starting to look more comfortable on the floor. Dance patterns and more complicated moves are becoming habit, and the nervousness that marks a beginner's face has evaporated from his own. After two more trips down the floor, the mixer closes, and David announces the week's anniversary and birthday celebrants. Four couples take the floor for the celebratory spotlight waltz, and after about one minute of dancing, David invites the rest in attendance to join them. So begins the second half of the dance.

Laurie is talking to David about waltz music when I return from the mixer. A lawyer, she also competes at the national level in amateur dance competitions with William as her partner. She is single now, but in a few years will marry a medical student she meets at the Regent. She is recognized as the best female standard dancer in regular attendance, though she is rivaled by another local competitor, Sophia, who, along with her dance partner Steve, also consistently place in competitions.

But tonight, Laurie is talking with David about waltz music, requesting that he play "a good one." This is part of an ongoing discussion, and David knows what her idea of "a good one" is. She prefers waltzes in which the triple meter is obscured by more complex counter melodies and inner voices. I think David agrees with her sensibility, but he also feels an obligation to the beginning dancers to play waltz music in which the triple meter is most clearly articulated with a heavy bass accent on beat one. Knowing she typically dances the second waltz of a set with her competition partner William, David searches for something Laurie will like. After the waltz and a quick "Thank you" nod to David, she spins on her heels, takes the hand of Herb, her competition partner for Latin dances, and heads to the floor for the cha cha. She and Herb have only begun to compete in the Latin dances, and it is not uncommon to see them talking about different moves, starting and restarting, while they work out different steps on the floor.

William stealthily slides his hand in mine and we head out to a spot on the dance floor for a rumba. William is a competition dancer in the smooth dances, but is not particularly adept at the Latin genres. Accustomed to the fixed torso of the waltz and the fluid placement of steps in the foxtrot, as if floating over the music, the Latin dances seem somewhat antithetical to his strengths. But William knows that I do not particularly enjoy dancing the rumba, nor am I any better at it than he, and I am happy to essentially slow dance, or sway gently in time to the music.

This has come to be a habit for us, but it took some initial negotiation. I sensed him tentatively trying to lead the more legitimate steps of the rumba, accommodating my knowledge of American to his familiarity with International style, and I responded unenthusiastically to leads for the more flashy moves indicative of the theatrical romantic tension at the core of rumba performance. At some point, he teased me gently until I confessed my ambivalence for the genre. He relaxed, understanding that he did not have to work so hard, and we settled into a slow, duple meter slow dance, a style that always seemed very "un-ballroom." We used the time to discuss our week. We fell into calling this dance "our rumba," and ever since we danced at least one at every Friday night dance, using the occasion to converse about the latest news and gossip.

William moved to Illinois decades ago, after a tour in military service, to complete a graduate degree in engineering. Before finishing his program, however, he started his own computer software developing company and never returned to school. He enjoys teaching dance on a volunteer basis for the Dancing Illini, and he might have enjoyed teaching in academia as well. So, while the regret at not having completed his doctorate is not overwhelming, it does seem to persist. William and his business partners are currently entertaining a buy-out offer from a major international technology icon, an offer that would make him a millionaire. While the offer is attractive, he worries about what he will do with his time. He is divorced, middle aged, and likes to stay busy. He has a number of hobbies, including ballroom dancing, race walking, and volunteer work for various charitable foundations. He also travels and participates in bicycle tours, this year to Scotland. He will eventually negotiate an offer in which he sells the company but stays on as manager for a number of years to ease the transition.

William is one of the most accomplished dancers at the Regent, and he is generous with his time and skills. Without any air of frustration, he will accommodate even the least-skilled partner. Though he often violates a central taboo of dancing—providing unsolicited advice or corrections to another—the gentle manner with which he does so and the fact that his skills are widely respected allows him to do so at the Regent with relative impunity.

William understands that his dance skills are capital at the Regent, and he invests this capital in attracting the youngest, most beautiful women for dance partnerships and occasionally romantic liaisons. Several women have reciprocated. "I understand," William once confessed, "that women use me for my dance skills and lead me on until I ask them out. Then when I do, they turn me down." I begin to wonder. Is he talking about me?

5
Joy, Flow, and Personal Transformation

Jane, the part-time Regent instructor, is a white, middle-aged mother of three boys. She is in excellent shape, her petite and athletic build a testament to the years she has spent as a competitive race walker and ballroom dance instructor. She and her husband, Mark, started dancing in 1996, about the same time I started this project, and I have followed them through the trajectory from beginners to advanced dancers and local teachers. When I asked her about those early days, about what brought her back to the ballroom week after week, she said: "The thing I enjoyed most about dancing was that I didn't have to think at all about it. It took me out of everything else in my mind. You know? So I was just enjoying the moment. I really needed that at that time."

The pleasure of social ballroom dance for most adults is due, in part, simply to the fact that the genre is a matter of choice for most of its participants. It is not compulsory as work, nor as an expression of familial, cultural, or community responsibility. As an affinity practice, it is perceived as being independent of the obligatory aspects of work and social life; it is an expression of play, leisure, and free time. The "leisure time" frame in which participation occurs is one contributing factor in its ultimate affect.[1]

The transition from everyday self to the dancing self takes place gradually as an individual enters the dance hall and is enveloped in the sound of dance music while he changes his shoes. During weekly classes, my male partners often commented with a deep sigh and shimmy of the shoulders that they needed to relax and let go of their work and family responsibilities. Others commented that they appreciated the fact that once class started, they just followed David's directions. As one male dancer stated, "I don't have to make any decisions. I'm not in charge of anything. I just do what David tells me to. It's nice for a change." This is the first stage in a more radical shift in awareness that occurs during the dance event itself, where purposeful movement and intense concentration cause feelings of self-consciousness and worry over everyday life to be displaced with feelings of joy, euphoria, and a particular kind of selflessness or the silencing of the internal critical voice that is active much of our waking hours. As Jane stated above, it took her out of "everything else in [her] mind" and to a place of enjoyment.

In his groundbreaking work on play and happiness, Mihaly Csikszentmihalyi provides us with a model for understanding the events that can lead to such states of awareness. I provide a brief summary here, as it is particularly appropriate for understanding the appeal of ballroom dance as play. His earlier work with musician Stith Bennett (1971) addresses the structural qualities of games and their potential for generating altered states of awareness. Subsequently, as he expanded the theory to include activities beyond games, he called this state "optimal experience" (Csikszentmihalyi and Csikszentmihalyi 1988) or "flow" (Csikszentmihalyi 1990).

Csikszentmihalyi and Bennett state that play is grounded in the "concept of possibility" (1971, 45) and is action that generates action, creating a unified experience flowing from one moment to the next. The authors focus their attention on heightened states of awareness and focus, those moments of being so completely absorbed in an activity that one feels lost in it, not reflecting on the rapid decision-making process that prolongs the activity and drives the fun. This acting in the moment, what the authors term, "voluntary fiat" or the "operational volition or decision for immediate action" (45), described by any layperson as "getting lost in the moment," is what leads to the engagement of play activities.

Ideally, the conditions for play are met when we achieve a balance between our abilities and the options available to us—"when we can make each action by voluntary fiat, but still do not exhaust possible actions" (46). Our everyday lives are beset with a large number of ongoing projects with a vast number of possibilities for action. Generally, in nonplay contexts, the number of possible outcomes is always considerably more than the one series of events that does occur. Juggling the number of ongoing projects in our lives and the countless options available leads to feelings of anxiety and worry, an imbalanced state not conducive to experiencing play. The opposite end of this spectrum, when conditions become routinized and monotonous, is marked by boredom (45–46). "The fewer opportunities for action we perceive, the more bored we become" (46). Both boredom and worry preclude the necessary conditions for play. Balance between the two is a necessary condition for optimal experience:

> Now we are able to conceptualize the experience of play. When there is a "balanced" state of affairs, when we can make each action by voluntary fiat, but still do not exhaust possible actions, the necessary conditions for play are established. The play experience is invoked when our action "resonates" with the environment; when "feedback" provides sufficient possibilities for an uninterrupted flow of action. *Play is experienced when it is impossible for the actor to differentiate projects available by voluntary fiat from assessed situational possibilities.* Awareness merges with action, and a play episode is begun. A most outstanding quality of this state of ambience or participation with the environment is the actor's lack of an analytic or "outside" viewpoint on his conduct: a lack of self-consciousness. (46, emphasis in original)

One measure of a good game or play activity, then, is its ability to sustain this state of awareness merged with action. Here, Csikszentmihalyi's notion of voluntary fiat and flow is useful for the analysis of musical events, where the temporal aspects of music force an out-of-time time continuum that simultaneously generates and structures the flow of one moment to the next as long as it sounds. Music, it seems to me, is a particularly powerful ingredient in generating flow states expressly because it helps establish alternative and perhaps more flexible senses of time such as those described by Csikszentmihalyi. He states, "Another common feature of flow experiences is a 'distorted' sense of time. When consciousness is fully active and ordered, hours seem to pass by in minutes, and occasionally a few seconds stretch out into what seems to be an infinity. The clock no longer serves as a good analog of the temporal quality of experience" (1988, 33). While the clock may no longer serve well in this capacity, music may provide an optimal opportunity for alternatively temporalizing experience. Coupled with dance, action that generates action, the two together are powerful instruments for generating flow states.

Csikszentmihalyi is not the first or only to note the affects of this kind of intense focus on our state of awareness, experience of pleasure, and well-being. Philosopher Charles Sanders Peirce's notion of "secondness," or relations between two entities without the mediation of a third, is particularly relevant here (1955, 1958, 1960, 1991, 1992; Lea 2001; Turino 1999). So too are the numerous postulations about meditation and trance states found across the academic disciplines, in practical theories of sport and athletics, and in self-help literature that highlight the importance of an object for attention—whether a mantra, visualized image, repetitive motion, or just one's own breathing—on which the mind focuses with the eventual goal of silencing the internal critical voice. Much of this work resonates with Csikszentmihalyi's concept of optimal experience and flow.

While many, including myself, focus on the advantages of such flow states, it is important to remember that there is a danger in projecting upon these states a belief in their inherent goodness (see, for example, Feld 1984; Keil and Feld 1994; Keil 1995; Turino 1993, 2008). Such music and dance structures are not necessarily an expression of the absence of social power (especially gender, which is often omitted in these discussions), nor are such feelings necessarily used toward ideal or egalitarian ends (Turino 2000; Turino and Lea 2004). Challenging the prevailing tendency to associate music grooves with egalitarian social structure, Ingrid Monson writes:

> I do not see grooves as necessarily egalitarian, but as often stratified musical textures in which people expect each other to fulfill particular roles—such as keeping time, walking, soloing—so that the greater good (a swinging, grooving whole) can emerge. . . . [T]he fact remains that the processual whole, more often than not, requires at least a temporary division of labor that may or may not be accompanied by differences in power, money, and prestige. . . . There is a difference between the feeling that getting into a groove can create (which can be, as Keil 1995 suggests, an incredible communal and experiential high) and the social organization of its production and circulation. However good various types of grooves may make us feel, in other words, they cannot be presumed to be innocent of power. (1999, 52)

Unlike the traditions to which Monson refers, the expression of power is more explicit, in both audible and visual ways, in ballroom dance. The genre is hardly subtle when it comes to articulations of social power. As such, it is understandable that those who believe groove, flow, and altered states to be expressions of deeper egalitarian structures might find it difficult to believe that the genre is capable of producing feelings of communitas, well-being, and connectedness.

It should also be noted that the work of psychologists and therapists on Adult Attention Deficit Hyperactivity Disorder suggests that hyperfocusing can be a problem for those who cannot exit such states when socially appropriate to do so. While I did no comprehensive data collection on this matter, it was my experience that a number of ballroom dancers did develop something akin to an addiction for the flow state induced by dancing that occasionally impeded their ability to develop meaningful social relationships with their dance partners. Rather than letting a dance relationship unfold slowly, getting to know one's partner and his or her boundaries, some dancers jumped into the dance at their own balancing point for voluntary fiat, to use Csikszentmihalyi's terminology, even if it was well beyond the ceiling of the partner. In such an event, the unwitting partner often left the dance feeling upset or "invisible" to her partner. There is a kind of tempo for establishing the conditions for and then entering flow states, and this tempo is somewhat unique to each person. Ballroom can accommodate such variety in "flow tempos," if you will, but the best dances are usually found between individuals whose flow tempos are similarly calibrated.

The conventions governing ballroom dance performance practice and pedagogy allow for the balance necessary for generating flow states to be easily achieved and maintained across a wide range of abilities, partnerships, and cultural contexts. The formulaic way in which moves are conceived, sequenced, and interchanged one for another allow for a slow expansion of the possibilities for action as the dancer develops his or her skills. While the limits for possibility are highly restricted at the outset in order to match the limited number of moves a beginner could employ, there is no perceivable limit to the ceiling of competence. The vista of possibilities opens to dancers as they learn the skills for responding to those possibilities.[2]

One could, in fact, interpret the entire history of ballroom dance pedagogy (for the layperson) and changes in its practice from its emergence in the late 1800s as being shaped by the desire to cultivate flow states within the changing cultural contexts of the twentieth century. In discussing her experiences as a dance reconstructionist, dance historian Linda Tomko describes the emotional affect of turn-of-the-century waltz: "Particularly remarkable is the sensation of ongoing flow achieved through coupled bodies, pursuing but not driven along the line of direction in the ballroom, bodies matching the ongoingness of the music's rhythmic drive, emphasizing affects of lightness and moderately sustained initiations of effort. These were among the experiences that turn-of-the-century waltzing afforded as the conventional standard for ballroom dancing" (1999, 24).

This historical development of pedagogy has led to a highly codified set of rules and conventions in contemporary practice. As noted in the following quote from Dean, the astrophysicist and occasional amateur competitor, ballroom dance is notorious even among its practitioners for being extremely restrictive:

> Ballroom dances live and die by a syllabus: common groups of figures choreographed, shaped, and aligned down to a gnat's ass. International ballroom is the ultimate realization of this. The upside is universality: a 3-step and feather in Int'l foxtrot looks the same anywhere in the world—sort of like a McDonald's Quarter Pounder with Cheese (personal communication, May 30, 2002).

The same qualities have been lampooned in feature films such as *Strictly Ballroom* and *Shall We Dance?* But, as Dean (and the films) suggest, this quality lends itself to greater potential for optimal experience among a greater number of individuals across a greater number of geographic regions. These rules are crucial in providing limits on the choices available to participants and for providing immediate feedback regarding how one is doing, both important factors in creating flow states (Csikszentmihalyi 1988, 32).

Csikszentmihalyi and Bennett (1971) conclude that play contexts are those in which social reality is not up for negotiation, those in which the "actors are absolutely bound to a limited set of actions and to identical accounts of those actions; play is a social system with no deviance" (56). Perhaps more important, "if given only a manageable number of options for action and an unambiguous symbol system, no viewpoint other than the player's viewpoint is necessary—the social self becomes superfluous, and the player can merge with the process in a state of monistic awareness" (56). Given this, it is not surprising that the lead/follow relationship is revered so highly among dance practitioners. Total acceptance of the lead/follow relationship, regardless of how politically troubling it may appear from outside of the dance frame, may be necessary for the achievement of optimal experience. It helps to explain, to some degree, the kind of re-signification and cognitive dissonance women and men express about the antiquated politics of the male-lead/female-follow convention. The structure of the relationship (lead/follow), critical to achieving flow states and for providing immediate feedback, is maintained but reframed to be on par with whatever contemporary gender politics happen to be. This is not to say, however, that the genre could not absorb a certain amount of social change—in particular, accepting a greater diversity of sexual orientations and same-sex partnerships—without violating the affective and time-honored tradition of lead/follow in which couple dance is embedded.[3]

Couple dancing presents many of the components of the games on which Csikszentmihalyi's theories were based. It is a world of restricted options, with immediate feedback in which one becomes entirely engrossed. For the leader, the split-second timing of suggesting a move, responding to your follower's response, considering the move that you are performing even as you are also considering the moves that will follow, all the while directing the momentum of your partnership in and around other couples in the throes of the same process has the equivalent thrill potential of a good play in hockey or the rush of rock climbing. The same goes for the follower, who attends with heightened awareness to every possible cue her partner may send (intentional and otherwise) and seeks to follow with near instantaneous reflex while avoiding the temptation to anticipate the next lead before her partner has a chance to perform it. Maintaining this fluid exchange of lead and follow within the quick timing demanded by the music is a fun challenge that absorbs and delights all of the senses. As Leo stated:

> For me, the joy is that I can go to a dance . . . and I can ask [someone] to dance, and when the music starts and we just move along together and its smooth and it feels good. It's amazing to me that it can really happen. The music is unforgiving; it goes along. And they don't know what I'm gonna do. And a lot of times, even with a woman I never met and who maybe even learned to dance someplace different and in a different style, and its amazing that it can work good and feel so good. Plus, when the dance is over, we can just say "Thank you very much" and be done with it. You can have this intense, . . . well, . . . to me it's intimacy.[4]

It does not always work this way of course. Not all partnerships lead to optimal experience. But, as dancers attested over and again, the promise of such an experience drives most to keep dancing until the next one occurs.

Flow and Becoming Beautiful

Throughout this text, individuals have attested to the transformative power of ballroom dance—whether the dance provided momentary escape from the mundane and painful realities of daily life, an opportunity to rebuild a marriage, or the possibility for rebirth as a more confident, healthy, and beautiful woman or man. These moments, the serious and occasionally self-deprecating references to transformation and escape, reveal the power of the performative perception and are suggestive of a real-world ache that remains otherwise concealed.

And so, while some might attribute the pleasure and feeling of well-being that ballroom dancers experience to the fact that the performance is merely entertainment—a trifle—or to the physical responses such cardiovascular activities elicit, I would suggest that flow states are more affective for the ways they come to signify in the social realm (Dyer 1992). It is not because they mean so little, but because they mean so much—literally, in that such affective states are dense with semiotic potential. How we make sense of these experiences (as they are occurring and after the fact) affects the ways we bring them about. For flow states do not happen to us: they are actively created and maintained by us. As such, they garner meaning with every occurrence and every reflection upon them. They are a manifestation of human energy, human investment, and human desire.

Flow states are marked by a kind of intense and sustained focus that silences the internal voice or running monologue that comments on everything the individual considers.

> Because of the deep concentration on the activity at hand, the person in flow not only forgets his or her problems but loses temporarily the awareness of self that in normal life often intrudes in consciousness, and causes psychic energy to be diverted from what needs to be done. . . . In flow, the self is fully functioning, but not aware of itself doing it, and it can use all the attention for the task at hand. At the most challenging levels, people actually report experiencing a *transcendence* of self, caused by the unusually high involvement with a system of action so much more complex than what one usually encounters in everyday life (Csikszentmihalyi 1988, 33, emphasis in original).

While it is a necessary part of being human, this internal voice can also prohibit well-being and have destructive effects on our lives. We use it to make decisions (perhaps less often than we think) and to make sense of the world around us. But it is often with this internal voice that we express (and subsequently hear) feelings of self-doubt and self-criticism, feelings we may try to conceal from people in our lives. This critical voice speaks not only the thoughts and belief structure of the self, but it speaks also on behalf of the society in which that self was raised. One distinguishing quality of flow experiences is that they are generally exempt from this voice. This is one of the reasons couple dancing and other such activities are pleasurable and beneficial; the heightened engagement that is a hallmark of optimal experience precludes criticism and commentary in the moment.[5]

Given this, it should not be surprising that American dancers testify to the fact that dancing makes them feel beautiful. The idea of beauty is inherently relational—it describes the perception of one by another and speaks directly to that which is socially valued. Challenges to our self-conception as beautiful stem primarily from our own feelings of self-doubt, our concerns over social acceptance and what other members of our social group think of us. Silencing these concerns, living completely without them in a state of "transcendence" for even a brief time, sets us on the path to self-acceptance and greater conviction in our own worth and beauty. Such a state, coupled with the biochemical "rush" that often results from aerobic activity, optimal experience, or being released from one's own internal critic through movement, makes dancers feel more than happy. They feel beautiful.

This feeling is substantiated by the movement itself. Optimal dance experiences take place when movement, momentum, and ideas move seamlessly, without reflection or critical awareness, between the two dancers, causing them to form one entity moving fluidly among others. Being lost in the moment with someone else in improvised but nevertheless tight synchrony signifies the kind of connectedness and social acceptance dancers desire, and it is often interpreted as material evidence of that connectedness—that is, the flow state generated from the actual physical connectedness of the dancers is often interpreted as proof of a social connection and proof of the potential to be connected (Hooper 1991; Peirce 1955; Turino 1999, 2008). In his discussion on Peircian semiotics and its utility in the analysis of music and dance, Turino states:

> Knowing and hence being able to perform appropriately in the style is itself a dicent index of belonging and social identity, because performance competence *is both a sign and simultaneously a product of* shared . . . knowledge and experience—shared habits. In music and dance performance a higher level of attention is placed on rhythm and synchrony; participants are acutely aware of the groove and their relation to it and through it their relation to the other participants. In participatory performances, feelings of social synchrony are at a higher level of focal awareness but still involve iconic and indexical signs which typically create effects of feeling and direct experience" (Turino 2008, 43, emphasis in original).

Or as married couple and college professors Chelsea and Norman described it:

> C: "There is something about moving together, to the music, that is so profound, very profound."
>
> N: "Yes, for me it is all about connection. Feeling that other person to the music. . . . I want to see people looking at each other and connecting. That's what I want to feel."

In his description of Irene Castle, Gilbert Seldes, the early-twentieth-century dance critic, suggests that optimal experience enhances the visual spectacle created by a dancing couple as well: "No one else has ever given exactly that sense of being freely perfect, of moving without effort and without will, in more than accord, in absolute identity with music" (Castle 1980, 87). Through dance, Irene Castle, the iconic figure of the genre, became perfect not through force, practice, or learnedness, but through freedom from effort and will.

Dancers have suggested, and I would agree that the meaning derived from this experience transcends the fleeting moments of flow states themselves. Feeling the potential for greater self- and social acceptance within a dance enables one to conceive of an everyday existence filled with such approval. In his discussion of social cohesion among diasporic communities, Thomas Turino suggests something similar when he states: "Artistic practices and experiences foreground the crucial interplay of the possible and the actual, an interplay that is, in fact basic to all experience and yet which often goes unnoticed. . . . Art foregrounds the interplay of the possible and the actual in a variety of ways and in so doing is not so much an 'imitation of life' as it is an emphatic version of this interplay: the very stuff of life. . . . [A]rt can make the possible and imaginary actual within an artistic frame, and by so doing help actualize the idea in daily life" (Turino and Lea 2004, 10–11).

Beauty is, of course, a culturally constructed notion that articulates the values of a society, or at least those of its dominant class. For America these values have been rooted in Western European cultural practice. Ballroom dance is one field in which these values have been articulated, constructed, and occasionally challenged and renegotiated. It is an expression of that which has been considered beautiful in America, in terms of the judgment of both art and people. The celebration of slim, white, heterosexual, upper-class bodies engaged in an artistic practice that employs physical control, elongated posture, concern for line, intentional movement, smoothness, artistic distance, and the dramatic portrayal of archetypal characters is not isolated to ballroom dance. Rather, ballroom dance reinforces these values—ideals merged in body, movement, and sound—in a profound affective moment that allows dancers not only to experience the interplay of the actual and the possible, but also to *be* that interplay of the actual and the possible.

My point here is that dancers do not only *feel* transformed by the experience, they *are* transformed, if only for the duration of a song. Then one song leads to a next, one night of dancing leads to another, and individuals slowly integrate new habits of being . . . experiencing moments of heightened focus and moving in unity with others without the internal critical voice that suggests change is not possible or that they are anything less than beautiful. This is the power of artistic practice, and perhaps the reason it exists at all.

Interlude

Many folks have standing partners for the last waltz of the evening, whether it be a spouse, a friend, or a competition partner. I have no arrangement and so take my chances week to week. Leo's standing partner is not here tonight, so he raises his brow, tilts his head toward the floor while holding out his hand, and we're heading together for the final waltz of the night. I walk into his arms without hesitation, feeling his torso with my own before setting up our frame for the waltz. Leo is one of my favorite partners, and I am more than happy to finish a great night of dancing with him.

Having worked as a physician for a number of years, Leo retired early, frustrated with the hassle of insurance companies and legal issues that required more of his time than caring for patients. He occasionally refers to himself as a "leftie." He lost his only brother in Vietnam, was beaten while registering southern black voters during the civil rights movement, and has been known, on occasion, to smoke a little hash. He is also a key informant for my work. This is due in part to the fact that he will eventually become very interested in salsa, the topic of my dissertation, but more so because I have recently purchased a house just around the block from his own bungalow.

It is good to be Leo's neighbor. He is one of the "old fashioned" neighbors from whom one can borrow sugar or, more likely, hedge trimmers. He offered me firewood as a house-warming present. He surveys my lawn to help me assess the health of my trees and to suggest new plantings. He is a member of the Urbana Tree Commission—a group I never knew existed. He likes tall, sturdy, old-fashioned trees, preferably with wide canopies—oak or beech. He doesn't want to be bothered with ornamentals or decorative shrubs. He is generous with his friendship and relaxing company to share a beer with.

It is forbidden to ever "drop by" Leo's home—yes, literally forbidden. He set down the ground rules for this as soon as I had my lawn furniture unpacked on the front porch of my bungalow just down the street from his own. He swears to be a terminal bachelor and hermit with an unusual flair for home decorating. While he suspects I may be one of the few women who could appreciate his eccentric taste, I will need some time for mental preparation. I suspect that it is Leo who needs the time to learn that I am trustworthy. I have danced with Leo for years, I have been his neighbor for one year, and he thinks we might be ready very soon.

When thinking over my relationship with Leo, I am reminded of the metaphor, albeit a tired one, comparing relationships to poker games. Over the past few years, Leo has methodically included me in his life, in incremental steps that I imagine he thinks culminate in an invitation to his home. At each stage he looks for me to match his investment. I do so willingly, without intensity—sharing honest thoughts about mutual friends, broken hearts, and my new boyfriend (and future husband), Christopher. Leo is skeptical of marriage, convinced he knows more miserable married people than miserable single people.

I, too, am a person who relishes privacy. But I have invited Leo to stop by my place whenever he pleases, knowing it will never be an inconvenience. We usually walk to the neighborhood sandwich shop, Sweet Betsy's, just down the block. Tonight it is to sample the premiere of the Mexican special—two chicken enchiladas, rice, and beans for $5.25. Christopher joins us. He has recently registered for introductory ballroom and salsa dance lessons. I listen while he and Leo talk about what it means to learn the lead parts. Leo is supportive of Christopher's desire to learn salsa, knowing that then the three of us can go out together. Unlike many ballroom-to-salsa converts, he likes to attend the salsa nights at local clubs rather than dancing only at the Regent, even though he feels out of place in many ways. Aside from an enthusiastic male heterosexuality, his age, race, language, and, most important, dance style mark him as different. The more friendly faces in the crowd the better.

Leo is no stranger to graduate school and dissertations, and he periodically inquires as to the progress on my own. He knows I am writing about dance, and he believes (correctly) that I am engaging some of the same issues he thinks about as well. I usually tell him what I am working through and occasionally ask his opinion. He has provided an invaluable sounding board for my thoughts about dance and its role in our lives:

"So, JB, what nonsense are you writing about these days?" he teases.

"I'm thinking about ethnicity. What do you think about it?" I tease back.

"First you tell me what you mean by it, and then maybe I'll tell you what I think." He replies with a wry but suspicious grin. Caught a bit off guard, I mumble and stutter something about not knowing what it really means but feeling it has some importance to dancers. When he is satisfied that he isn't about to be trapped into incriminating himself, he interrupts with enthusiasm.

"Well, then, if you ask me what I think of ethnicity," he said, "I am against it! I know the Latinas I dance with don't understand my dancing, and they rarely take the time to learn about it either. They might actually find they like it. But I know they are offended that I combine salsa with the other dances I know. You know me, you know my style. They think I'm stealing their dance, or that I don't appreciate what it means to them. And I know America has a history of riding roughshod with our Sherman tanks all over Third World countries, and I hate it. But I just want to dance." The discourse of ethnicity, it seems, makes it difficult. He continued, "Many people think that what I do is not salsa [dancing], and that's o.k. with me. So to make it easy, I do not call it that. I give them that. I simply tell people that I love to dance to salsa music." The distinction allows for anyone to label Leo's somewhat unique, syncretic salsa dance style what they will without controversy. No arguments over authenticity, no feelings of guilt over issues of ownership and appropriation.

But tonight we are dancing the last waltz of the night, and David plays a vocal number—an uncharacteristic choice for the last waltz of the night. Leo is one of the few partners who does not mind my singing along. Interestingly, talking to one another during a dance is not uncommon, but it's not something Leo tolerates easily, so he is happy that I will occupy myself with the lyrics, ". . . I was dancin' . . . with my darlin'. . . ." Leo's face communicates the intensity with which he engages the dance. His muscles are tight, eyebrows raised, lips pursed as he leads us from a twinkle, with me stepping across his body from his left arm to the right, and it is clear he is thinking about the next sequence of moves. We weave in and between the other dancers, all in step and turning independently and together at one moment, knitting a complex and loopy pattern on the floor.

Regardless of what genre he is dancing, Leo's torso is quiet. His knees are active and he holds his hands at a forty-five-degree angle from his body. Whether a waltz, a swing, or a salsa, Leo's style depends more on body flight, on moving through space quickly in balance, and though the patterns are different between the different genres, the style is the same. It isn't regulation ballroom style. It feels nice.

As is often the case when I smooth dance with Leo, I experience a moment, I don't know how long, of just disappearing. Moving fluidly throughout my physical world so perfectly in sync with my partner, the other couples, and the space around me. It requires no intention. I let go, forget myself and what it feels like when my material existence meets with the resistance of other forces and decisions must be made. The audience of fellow dancers is a blur of color and no longer present a critical gaze that reminds me that I, myself, am visible. I've stopped singing, but I don't remember doing so, and for some time my own internal monologue, including my ethnographer's critique, is quieted as well. For a few short moments I am lost, and it feels delightful. What a gift.

I am awakened by the closing refrains of the song. Leo has a keen musical sensibility, and it is clear that he is matching the dance phrase we are creating to the musical phrase. He moves toward me, into my body, signaling the point turn that is his hallmark. I move toward him and we are poised together, turning as one entity, sharing a single center of gravity between my right leg and his left. We continue to turn together as the final cadence of the song sounds. "That was nice," he says, as he pats me on the back and we head off the floor together. Indeed, it was.

Appendix

BALLROOM CANON

This section contains a brief survey of the many genres performed in my fieldsite. Each ballroom dance genre emerged and was codified at a specific historical moment, continued to develop within a large-scale hierarchical organization, and exists today in a complex relationship to this history. Although alike in numerous ways, each genre signifies something distinct and provides a unique experience for dancers today. Hence, while comprehensive coverage of each genre individually does not fall within the scope of this work—for a book could be written about each one—a brief introduction of the distinguishing features of each is helpful for understanding the relationship between the various genres.

The picture presented here is primarily informed by performance at my fieldsite—a social ballroom dance studio and performance venue in a midwestern college town. In many instances, there is variability from one context and studio to another, between competition social practice, and among geographic regions. I have privileged my fieldsite and social dance more generally, as this book cites the numerous academic sources available to the reader that privilege competitive practice.

First, however, I would like to include a brief point about music and tempo, which is an important factor in dance music. Each official dance organization has published a recommended tempo for each genre, articulated in measures per minute (as opposed to beats per minute, which is standard in Western music notation). Performances that are advertised as being in "strict time" are

Table 2: Competition tempo requirements for the IDSF and USABDA.

	USABDA		IDSF
Standard	*International*	*American*	*International only*
Waltz	30	28–30	30
Tango	33	30–32	33
Viennese waltz	60	54–56	60
Foxtrot	28	30–32	30
Quickstep	52		50
Latin			
Cha cha	32	28–30	30
Samba	50	54–56	50
Rumba	27	32	27
Bolero	24		None
Paso doble	62		62
Jive	34–38 (jive, Lindy, East Coast)		44
West Coast swing	28–32		None
Club	No International/American distinction		
Hustle	28–30		None
Mambo	47		None
Merengue	29–32 (in 4/4)		None
Salsa	No MPM recommendation other than slightly slower than mambo.		None

those that fall within conventional tempo regulations for each genre and do not fluctuate in tempo.

Table 2 shows the recommended ranges for the various dances by the United States of America Ballroom Dance Association (USABDA) and the International DanceSport Federation (IDSF), the two organizations that dominated U.S. national competition practice during the time of my fieldwork. As stated above, these organizations have been retooled as the World DanceSport Federation.

The Standard or Modern (International Style) or Smooth Dances (American Style) (also known as Standard Dances or Modern Dances)

Regent dancers used the terms "Modern," "Standard," and "Smooth" interchangeably, while dancesport competitors use the term "Smooth" to refer to the American style variants of this category and "Standard" to refer to International style. The term "Modern," the predecessor to "Standard," is a holdover from the early twentieth century (when couple dances were modern compared to the line dancing of the previous age) and is no longer endorsed by the DanceSport Federation. Interestingly, while the three terms were treated as synonyms by most Regent dancers, they most often used "Modern," as one can see from the interview quotes included this book. To minimize confusion between dancesport and social dance, I have used "Standard" most often in my prose, but direct quotes feature the term used by the speaker. This category includes the waltz, Viennese waltz, tango, foxtrot, and quickstep; they are all traveling dances, indicating that the couple travels counterclockwise around the dance floor in closed position. These genres make some, albeit quite limited, use of open position.[1]

WALTZ

The waltz, the oldest ballroom dance performed today, is believed to have emerged from a particular move (the valse) in French quadrille line dances (Aldrich 1991). At the time, the round dance (called as such because the couples move around the perimeter of the dance floor independently) was considered scandalous for the intimate position and privacy it afforded the couple. The earliest incarnation demanded almost constant spinning in one direction, causing performers to lose their balance, experience vertigo, or otherwise find themselves in compromising positions. Viennese waltz, a style of waltz performed by more advanced social dancers, most closely resembles this earlier style, although it has incorporated a reverse turn that allows the couple to change directions. It is performed at a fast tempo in 6/8 meter with sweeping strings (in the Straussian tradition) and is indeed difficult for social dancers to perform without falling off balance or out of time.

Immediately after the waltz emerged as an independent genre in the 1800s, dance masters began modifying the dance to make it more acceptable for public consumption. The standard competition waltz performed today is a product of this modification—including a slower tempo, 3/4 meter, and altered step design, which allows couples to move without turning at all, if they desire. The waltz music repertory consists largely of orchestral string arrangements of a range of melodies, some dating to the earlier part of the twentieth century and others newly composed. To create a more intimate sound, piano has been incorporated into some examples in lieu of the more grandiose orchestra. These were often commented upon by Regent dancers as being particularly nice for anniversary waltzes and the ritual last waltz of the evening. Occasionally, David would play popular music waltzes, such as "Tennessee Waltz" or Barbara Streisand's "Send in the Clowns," but these were used with care and usually not more than one per evening. On one of the few occasions when I acted as deejay for the Tuesday night practice dances, a few older couples remarked to me that they did not like the waltzes with lyrics and preferred the "classic" (instrumental) recordings.

TANGO

This dance of Argentine origins made its way to the United States through Paris and now holds a place as one of the most classic dances in the ballroom. Although the dance style has been significantly modified since its adoption in the first decades of the twentieth century, it continues to provide a vehicle for the highly stylized portrayal of dramatic exoticism and sexual struggle. The dance is relatively incompatible with bandoneon-based tango music from Argentina (as is now popular in the world music market), and performers of this style dance to music produced specifically for ballroom tango dancers. This specialized kind of tango music evokes the march-like character of the early twentieth century accompaniment and matches the stiff but dramatic quality of the ballroom tango. Snare drums punctuate a heavy, metronomic duple meter while large orchestral strings and winds perform sweeping melodies. Most recently, arrangers of ballroom music have begun to add the timbre of the bandoneon to their ballroom arrangements to capitalize on the recent mainstream popularity of the Argentine tango (see Goyena 1994; Savigliano 1995; Taylor 1976; Veloz and Veloz 1938).

FOXTROT

The origins of this dance are unclear. Some sources suggest that it was introduced by professional cabaret dancer Harry Fox, but others have also claimed ownership, including Vernon and Irene (Castle and Castle 1914; Malnig 1992; Stearns and Stearns 1968), while some theories suggest the foxtrot is a holdover from the animal dances in the early twentieth century. It was popular with exhibition and social dancers by about 1915. The movement is perfectly suited to music with a 4/4 meter and with the bass outlining beats one and three, employing a moderate tempo, swung eighth notes, and a vocal or instrumental melody. Classic examples are 1930s jazz standards and performances by jazz singers such as Frank Sinatra and Tony Bennett. The basic step once included a lateral step that upset the forward momentum of the dance. This side step appears to have been eliminated from all but beginning levels of American foxtrot.

At the Regent Ballroom, David Lin teaches students how to alternate between the American and International basic (exclusively for the foxtrot), an option that offers more rhythmic variation and stylistic diversity. This practice is not acceptable in competitions, and to my knowledge it is not common at other dance studios.

QUICKSTEP

Related to the foxtrot, this faster cousin emerged in the 1920s and is performed to show tunes, Tin Pan Alley, and other popular songs from the first half of the twentieth century, such as "Those Lazy, Hazy, Crazy Days of Summer," a popular choice at the Regent. Stylistically, this fast-paced round dance and its accompanying music are characterized by the depiction (if not romanticization of) youthful exuberance associated with the Roaring Twenties. The dance employs a physically demanding style of movement that includes running steps, skips, hops, and gallops associated with child's play. With elongated posture and large frame, couples travel the floor while incorporating a relatively high number of syncopated steps, including the aforementioned skips, hops, and jumps that are found only in this genre. It is perhaps the least prestigious of the Standard category dances, in part because of its corresponding music, which is valued very little today. Whereas waltz is performed to instrumental music perceived to be "classical," and foxtrot is performed to "jazz" (a newly emergent classical repertory of sorts), the popular songs of Quickstep, marked by their old-fashioned earnest jubilation, melodies, and duple meter (with accents on one and three and no backbeat emphasis), seem less culturally relevant than the other genres.

The Latin Dances

Regent dancers used the label "Latin" dances to refer to this category, regardless of whether they performed American or International style. DanceSport has codified the terms "Latin" and "Rhythm" for International and American style respectively, but Regent dancers rarely adhered to DanceSport regulations for their categorical terminology. Throughout this work I have used the term "Latin" because that is the language that prevailed at my fieldsite to refer to this category, which includes paso doble, rhumba/rumba, cha cha, samba, and jive or East Coast swing. These are spot dances, meaning that the couple does not travel around but remains basically fixed at one point, or spot, on the floor. They also contain many steps in open position.

PASO DOBLE

Considered Spanish in origin, this dramatic dance is performed strictly in competition. Evoking the mood and drama of a bullfight, the man is the matador and the female is his cape personified. The movement of the dance is intended to depict the motion of the cape as the bullfighter wields it to attract and escape the attention of the bull. I have never once witnessed the performance of this dance in any other context but competition or exhibition dances.

R(H)UMBA

This is another genre for which there exists an entirely different footwork pattern for the International and American styles, and while the rhythm of weight changes is somewhat different, it is possible to draw a relationship between them. Like the cha cha, weight changes are performed differently, with a significant emphasis on the placement and degree of bend in the knee. Both styles of rumba are perceived to be slow, romantic dances, performed to ballads with 4/4 meter, lyrical melody, and lush orchestration (often string orchestra), with limited Latin hand percussion timbres pushed to the fore of the musical texture. Solo vocalists are frequently used but are not a defining features of the genre. In competition, performers are compelled to convey a sense of intense, if not tragic, love through dramatic facial expressions and other theatrical gestures not commonly found in social dance situations.

At the Regent, American rumba was taught in all classes, but a number of advanced dancers, those who had taken private lessons or studied with the Dancing Illini, also knew the International style. To distinguish between them it was common to hear American-style rumba called "Rumba," and International style called "Bolero," even though in competition contexts the terminology is reversed. The history of the genre dates to the first half of the twentieth century, when American tourists were introduced to folkloric versions of Cuban rumba, an Afro-Cuban dance genre significantly different in style (see Daniel 1995; Moore 1995, 1997).

There is some degree of confusion about the different spellings, "rumba" and "rhumba." It was not uncommon, until recently, to find the ballroom genre spelled with the added "h," while "rumba" usually marked the specifically Afro-Caribbean styles. However, it appears that the spelling with the "h" has fallen out of favor by most ballroom dancers as well—perhaps because it signified too great a distance from the genre's original Latin predecessors. I have not found any definitive explanation for the origin of the alternate spellings.

CHA CHA CHÁ

The cha cha chá originated in New York's Latino communities during the mid-twentieth century as a variation on the mambo and continues to be a favorite (see Waxer 1994). Musical features include a 4/4 meter, layering of Afro-Caribbean ostinato patterns in straight eighth notes, including the signature accents on four-and-one (the "cha cha chá"), the incorporation of a clave pattern, and a syncopated bass line, all serving as the ground for a vocal or instrumental melody. It is not uncommon to find an expanded wind section in the typical Latin jazz band instrumentation and jazz-styled solos performed by individual instrumentalists. In terms of the movement, the difference between American and International styles is not in the basic rhythm of weight change but in the subtle difference in the style of weight change (in other words, how and when the knee is bent).

Regent dancers usually abbreviated the name of this genre to "cha cha," and I have taken to doing so throughout this text, which, in addition to reflecting contemporary practice, provides a rhetorical way of distinguishing it from its counterpart as performed in Latin American contexts.

Recordings for this genre are often culled from Latin dance bands of the 1950s as well as newly recorded Latin popular music, but ballroom competitions more often than not rely on strict-tempo ballroom recordings that imitate some aspects of the musical style with a simpler and more foregrounded rhythmic component. This type of music is especially popular for the beginning dancers, who commonly find the cha cha to be the most rhythmically difficult dance, and who struggle with the placement of the dance step within the music. The "cha cha cha" should fall on beats four-and-one within a 4/4 meter, but it is frequently misplaced on the downbeat of the measure (one-and-two).

SAMBA

Originating in Brazil, the samba made its way to the United States in the 1930s following a wave of interest engendered by the popularity of Carmen Miranda. The ballroom version of the genre bears little, if any, resemblance to contemporary samba dance style popular in Brazil today, although ballroom musical examples borrow some of the characteristic features, such as the prevalent duple meter with strong accent on beat two, dense textures, and certain timbral references to Afro-Brazilian samba school instruments, especially the cuíca, surdo, whistle, and pandeiro.[2] Samba is one of the most difficult ballroom dances to master, as it requires stylized arm gestures and upper-body flexibility, fast footwork, and an ability to hear the placement of very quick steps in the music. It is my observation that the greatest disparity between competition and social ballroom dancers is perceptible in the samba.

SWING

"Swing" is an umbrella term for a number of different American dance styles originating in the 1930s (swing, Lindy-hop, jive, and the like). Although the earliest association of the Lindy was with the black American youth community with whom it originated, swing was soon altered to be more accessible to white American youth.

East Coast swing, a competition dance, has a six-beat basic and has incorporated many of the rhythmic and stylistic qualities of the 1930s Lindy (which uses an eight-beat basic) and jive (which uses a six-beat basic). A spot dance making equal use of both open and closed positions, some versions include athletic jumps, kicks, and lifts, while others are more subdued in nature. The basic pattern of movement is similar between all East Coast styles, regardless of the rhythm of the basic, and social dancers perform them to the same music. At the Regent, the term "East Coast swing" referred exclusively to the six-beat pattern and was generally performed with a more subdued style than is typical of contemporary Lindy or jive dancers. Big band classics from the 1930s and 1940s are the mainstay of this repertory, supplemented with more recent swing hits such as those performed by Brian Setzer and the Stray Cats or the Cherry Poppin' Daddies.

A slightly modified version of the basic has been created for extremely slow tempi, as is common with 12/8 shuffle blues. Known as triple swing, the slow steps of the basic East Coast are subdivided into what is called a triple step. A Nightclub dance called West Coast swing was also developed in the last half of the twentieth century and is generally performed to music that employs the blues style complex, though many slow, 6/8 songs will work as well. The footwork is longer and more rhythmically complex than most other ballroom genres, allowing for the highest degree of improvisation on the part of both lead and follower. It is not generally danced in formal ballroom competition Latin heats, but as with the hustle, West Coast swing dancers have formed a national circuit for their own dance workshops and competitions.

The Nightclub Dances

Nightclub dances are those that are currently popular in nightclub settings, have their recent history in nightclubs, or can translate easily into the context of a nightclub. The colloquial term for this category at my fieldsite was "street dances." It generally served as a type of "catchall" for couple dance genres that local dancers enjoyed performing but that were not part of the competition syllabus; as such, the style was less standardized and codified than the others. Generally, nightclub dances do not constitute formal competition categories on the ballroom circuit unless the competition features a nightclub heat, which is not standard but can happen in regional contexts. At my fieldsite, nightclub dances were most often performed during the intermissions of formal organized ballroom events and included the Nightclub two-step (not at all similar to country or Texas two-step), hustle, West Coast swing, and most recently salsa, merengue, and on rare occasion, the bachata. When I first began my fieldwork, the polka was also included in this category, but over the course of the subsequent years it fell out of fashion completely (for more on polka, see Keil 1992). The cottage industry of ballroom dance music does produce some recordings of songs produced specifically for the performance of these genres within ballroom dance contexts, but at my fieldsite it was common for ballroom dance deejays to bypass this option and instead cull their selections from popular radio hits.

HUSTLE

Born out of the disco movement of the 1970s, the hustle was popularized by John Travolta in a stylized performance for the hit film Saturday Night Fever and by songs like Van McCoy's "Do the Hustle." It is still popular among a small but dedicated following who gather at hustle conventions throughout the country. These hustle aficionados, many of whom also dance ballroom and other couple dances, host their own competitions. A number of contemporary ballroom dancers and non-Latin salsa dancers initially became interested in couple dancing because of their involvement in the disco-era hustle movement. Stylistically, the hustle, like West Coast swing, is considered a "slot dance," meaning that the couple remains in one long, narrow space on the floor, moving back and forth in an elastic motion within this "slot."

This genre emphasizes smoothness, horizontal motion, and straight, vertical lines—with little bending of ankle, knee, or waist. There is no rise and fall in this genre, for dancers should always remain at the same height to emphasize the horizontal movement of the dancers' bodies. Disco music or disco remakes and covers are still the favored music for this dance, and given the cult popularity of this genre, it is not difficult to find.

I once spent a long night talking about hustle music with Matthew. While spinning his favorite selections on his home stereo, he passionately argued that hustle music should not be limited to the disco hits of the 1970s but should incorporate the wealth of house music being produced today in the United States and abroad. He played recordings recently purchased in South Asia, suggesting that they were more fun to dance the hustle to and possessed the potential to bring a new generation of dancers to the genre.

MAMBO

Reaching its height during the 1950s, the mambo is now out of favor in U.S. Latin clubs and seems to be most frequently performed today by ballroom dancers. The genre occasionally enjoys a brief resurgence of popularity, often in name only, as happened during my fieldwork with the release of Lou Bega's hit, "Mambo #5." Stylistically, the dance is a forerunner of the cha cha chá and a distant relative of salsa as well. Mambo is characterized by sharp movements—fast steps framed by stillness. It is similar to both cha cha chá and tango in this regard.

While most genres are definitively placed in one or another category, there are a few whose placement is more ambiguous; mambo is such an example. Depending upon context, the mambo can be included in competitions, but it does not hold a fixed place that many of the others do. It was performed in nightclub sets at the local collegiate competition, is not performed in the International style, and can be included in American heats. It is not uncommon to see it performed by competitors in exhibition events.

Because of its similarities to salsa in both sound and movement, a number of Regent couples danced salsa to what was listed on the dance card as mambo (see salsa entry for transcription). It is possible but perhaps more difficult to do the reverse. Salsa music has little impetus for the sharp, kinetic accent on beat 2, which is an identifying characteristic of the mambo.

NIGHTCLUB TWO-STEP

The origin of this dance is obscure. In some ways, it is simply a formalized version of what in some contexts is simply called "slow dancing" to popular love ballads. Popular songs during my fieldwork were Paul Young's "Every Time You Go Away" (from *Secret of Association*), Toni Braxton's "Let it Flow" (from *Secrets*), and Madonna's "Take a Bow" (from *Something to Remember*). The dance is coupled with other Nightclub genres like the hustle in the Regent's set list, but it is virtually never used in competition, often serving as an informal break between sets of ballroom standards and is not at all alike or related to the country two-step, a popular couple dance performed to country music.

SALSA

Though salsa originated in the Latin American neighborhoods of New York City, its most obvious musical roots are in Cuba. In the United States, the genre has been embraced by Latin American immigrants as a marker of pan-Latino identity, and over the past two decades salsa has become popular among non-Latin cosmopolitans. Although the dance is stylistically different from the mambo, of interest is the fact that the basic pattern and rhythm of the footwork is similar except that the rhythm is displaced by one beat. Whereas the mambo "breaks" (or begins) on beat 2 of the measure, salsa generally breaks on beat 1. Though many salsa songs are quite fast in tempo, the tempo can vary. In Latin American contexts, virtuosity, including frequent use of spins and the creation of original moves, are highly esteemed. Commercially recorded salsa music is used for both salsa dance clubs and ballroom dance contexts, though some ballroom dancers struggle with the rhythmic complexity and fast tempos of certain salsa examples.[3]

NOTES

INTRODUCTION

1. This scene is available for viewing on YouTube at http://www.youtube.com/watch?v=wLChx194rgY.

2. *Dancing with the Stars* encapsulates in dramatic form the very essence of what it is to become beautiful—what my informants, and apparently millions of viewers, find so compelling about the genre. The reality television show follows the transformation of beginner dancers (individuals who, for the most part, do not self-identify as dancers in any way) as they immerse themselves in the steps and conventions of the genre, becoming, in essence, Pygmalion figures in the process. The journey of these novices lies at the center of the show's dramatic arc, and Americans are invited to join the narrative by voting to keep their favorite stars dancing for another week. As I watched the first weeks of the first season of *Dancing with the Stars,* I sat dumbfounded that this idea made it past the pitch stage and into production. I anticipated a quick demise: "There just aren't enough people interested in ballroom dancing to make this work," I thought to myself. I could not have been more wrong. On further reflection and after hours spent viewing subsequent seasons, I see that the series brilliantly amalgamates of the dramatic elements of the two usually clearly demarcated worlds of ballroom performance—dancesport competition and social ballroom dance—into one dancing couple. *Dancing with the Stars* thus exploits and capitalizes on the most compelling aspects of both types of performance.

The show also incorporates the theater and spectacle that define competitive ballroom practice: virtuosic displays, sensational costumes, and, through high-stakes public performance, judging, and weekly elimination, the drama inherent in competitions. It features B-list celebrities (actors, athletes, politicians, or other notorious public figures and popular culture oddities) who enact the drama of beginning dancers, making themselves both vulnerable and more human as they step into the ballroom, for the very first time, on national television. The broadcasts include clips of these novices' practice sessions, showing their frustration with mastering the steps and the euphoria experienced when they successfully complete a routine, along with their personal testimonies about how ballroom dancing has changed their lives for the better. The power of ballroom dance, of performance, transforms these beginners, rendering them more beautiful to the viewing audience.

As if this were not enough drama, early seasons of the show also highlight the journey of one viewer who is given free lessons and, after weeks of studying, performs a routine on the show. Through video testimonies the individual explains how ballroom performance has raised her self-esteem, improved her physical fitness, and changed her life in other positive ways.

Of course, *Dancing with the Stars* is not the first dramatic portrayal of becoming beautiful through dance. Over the past thirty years, Hollywood dance films such as *Dirty Dancing, Take the Lead, Dance with Me,* and *Shall We Dance?* have also featured what I have elsewhere called the "transformation trope" (Bosse 2007b) within the context of ballroom dancing. But the rise of reality-television programming allowed *Dancing with the Stars* to depict the personal transformations of actual individuals rather than of fictional characters, thereby affirming for viewers the truth-value of the transformation narrative in an even more powerful and convincing way.

3. I depart from Victor Turner and Edward Bruner in two important ways. The first regards their foundational distinction between experience and expression. Their work draws upon storytelling, ritual, and visual arts, but it fails to engage performance, which, in participatory contexts is often simultaneously the experience and the expression. In the case of ballroom dance, performance is, in one moment, both an experience and an articulation about that experience. The dichotomy Turner/Bruner have created, itself an attempt to shun previous structuralist dichotomies, is useful in some areas of cultural life, but it does not stand so well in those involving performance. I have found the distinction useful for making sense of the narrative "becoming beautiful" and employ it to the degree that it provides an analytical framework for how people talk about their performance. But I, like many interested in the ethnomusicology of experience, seek to address how performance is a singular experience that encompasses multiple frames of knowledge, individual and shared understandings, and many aspects of articulation and self-reference that are not easily captured by the duality of the categories experience and expression. I think this is one area where ethnomusicologists, ethnochoreologists, and performance studies scholars are poised to make a significant contribution to the literature on experience.

The second way in which I diverge from Turner and Bruner is in their understanding of habits, what they term the "duller, more mundane aspects of culture," which, they argue, are in opposition to their "aesthetic expression in performance." "Cultures, I hold, are better compared through their rituals, theaters, tales, ballads, epics, operas than through their *habits*" (1986, 13, italics in original). This distinction fails to understand that which performers in the arts are painfully aware, that aesthetic expression, even the most unique and exceptional, is deeply rooted in repetition and routine. The work undertaken by performers is to more deeply ingrain habits that will be of use in novel performances. The dance itself is not novel, but the cumulation of practice, time, study, reflection, analysis, viewing, moving, and so on, in an effort to merge new ideas into habits. Artistic performances do not exist beyond or outside of habits: they are an utmost expression of habits. On this point, I join Bourdieu and other practice social theorists who argue that practice (habits) are an important source of cultural knowledge and are deeply connected to collective and individual identities. Ballroom dancers knew this as well, and they sought to establish new habits in order to create a new sense of self, or what I have called the "self-imaginary."

4. For examples, see the work of Tomie Hahn (2007), Katherine Hagedorn (2001), and Michelle Kisliuk (1998).

5. Personal names used for participants in this study are pseudonyms with the exception of David and Ellen Lin, owner-operators of the Regent Ballroom and Banquet Center.

6. The sensibility of the dancers I worked with resonated with my own understanding of identity construction as processual and performative. As such, my work owes a great debt to practice and performance theorists working in the latter half of the twentieth century, including scholarship by Bourdieu (1977) and Bauman (1971, 1977), as well as Butler's ([1990] 1999) groundbreaking work on performativity. See also Grossberg (1992); Giddens (1979); Hymes (1972); Turino (2008); Turino and Lea (2004). Also influential is the work of Charles S. Peirce (1955), whose theories of semiosis resonate with those of practice theorists in beneficial ways.

7. Increasingly, ballroom dance classes are available to children, and with the ramping up of children's ballroom competitions this trend is likely to continue. None of the dancers I worked with began ballroom dancing as children competitors, although a few of the older dancers did come of age during the swing era and learned to dance in the context of their contemporary youth culture. Some public schools across the United States have introduced ballroom dance in physical education classes, alongside square dancing and other recreational activities. These styles are notorious for being "out of touch" with the kinds of dancing children actually enjoy. None of the dancers I worked with came to the ballroom because they were excited by their middle-school physical education introduction.

8. The group of dancers I worked with shared a class-based cosmopolitan sensibility that obscured the diversity of the genre's participants in terms of race, ethnicity, or nation (see also Bosse 2007; Comaroff and Comaroff 1993; Erlman 1993; Guilbault 1993; and Turino 2000).

9. Ethnomusicological work on affinity groups include Gage Averill (2003), Slobin (1993), and Lausevic (2007), all of whom use the term "affinity group." Thomas Turino's (2008) work on old-time music and dance uses the term "cultural cohort" (111–16).

10. These figures were drawn from the U.S. Census 2000 and reflect the demographics during the time of my fieldwork.

11. My gratitude to Deb Busche for recommending the Regent so many years ago and for handing me off to her dance partner, Jeff Grossman.

12. Although conducting ethnography "at home," I do not consider it to have been "insider ethnography," two terms that are often used interchangeably (Aguilar 1981; Messerschmidt 1981; Moffatt 1992; Strathern 1987). I was a newcomer to ballroom dance, and I engaged the study of the genre in much the same way as any ethnomusicologist undertakes her research. Furthermore, although my status as an academic allowed me entrance into the world of the middle and upper classes, it was an uneasy one. As a first-generation college student raised in a large, working-class family, the world of higher education in which my newfound middle-class status was won felt foreign. As the investment mounted—dance classes, private lessons, cover charges, more appropriate clothing, and dance shoes—my aforementioned dance partner, who hoped to take hours of expensive private lessons per week, became frustrated with my inability to financially keep pace. Doubts about my literal self-worth and ability to successfully complete the project riddled my earliest days in the field.

While there were a small number of working-class dancers (fewer than 5 percent), most were at least middle class, and many were members of the local intellectual, political, and economic elite. The ballroom was not unlike the golf course as a site for professional as well as personal networking. Dancers planned luxurious travel vacations and cruises together, and validated the purchase of luxury goods: "Hey Susie, is that your new Jaguar in the parking lot? It's a beauty." David enjoyed trading stock tips and financial strategies with my first dance partner during our private lessons. Ballroomers occasionally suggested that their own financial and professional successes were the product of "hard work" rather than the chance of birth. When I once suggested, in good humor, that hard work has little to do with wealth, I was teased me for my liberal and unrealistic political beliefs.

Such feelings are not uncommon for those conducting fieldwork among local elites. George Marcus reports that few social scientists have viewed themselves as members of the elites they have studied, and most have felt as much outsiders as anthropologists were to the more traditional subject of tribal societies. This outsider status has created a bias toward connecting elite organizations to larger system frameworks and institutions with which they are often associated, and impeded more traditional aims of subjective culture and small group processes (1983, 9–17). The lack of coverage of the internal subcultures of elites, as opposed to the more common structural or institutional perspective, is due to the ideological and historical roots from which the elite research tradition has grown. "Much of elite research has been based on the presumption that we already know what elites are about, and that priority attention should be given to their social impact" (19). This book attempts to redress this bias, providing a glimpse of the personal lives, leisure activities, and subjective experiences of members of the middle and upper classes.

13. For notable exceptions, see Gage Averill's work on American barbershop singers (2003); Mirjana Lausevic's book on Balkan folk dancing in the United States (2007); and George Marcus's edited collection on the ethnographic study of elites (1983).

CHAPTER 1. THE CLASSIFICATION OF STYLE

1. During my years at the Regent, I can recall only two other men who elected to dance against the grain of consensus. One, like Pete, was very delicate in the manner in which he did so and very selective with his partners for such moments. The other was less so, and received harsh judgment from his peers for his actions.

2. The Australian comedy *Strictly Ballroom* (1992) is but one of several feature films to lampoon ballroom's "strict" adherence to regulation in many aspects of its performance.

3. The use of status distinctions, pervasive in ballroom dance, is one way that class differences find expression: they are "sublimated and legitimated through the powerful ideology of individual qualities of talent, merit, and giftedness" (Swartz 152).

4. See Bourdieu (1984) for more on taste and the symbolic dimensions of class.

5. Ballroom's routine references to ballet and other European high-art traditions are one significant indicator of its middle-class aestheticism (Bourdieu 1984). "Unlike the working class, the petite bourgeoisie enters the game of distinction but has neither the capital nor the corresponding habitus to appropriate fully dominant-class lifestyles. It attempts to emulate the standards set by the dominant class, but its 'striving towards distinction' betrays an awkward pretension where the dominant aesthetic displays ease and familiarity in the world of culture" (Swartz 176–77). Paradoxically, the efforts to elevate beyond one's middle-class status through ballroom performance (Bourdieu's "drive towards distinction") was a very articulation of that middle-class status.

6. This was not always true of the Arthur Murray and Fred Astaire Studios. Early in their existence they promoted social dance primarily as a means for upward mobility rather than virtuosic theater. McMains (2006) suggests it was in the 1960s and the firm establishment of solo rock dance in popular culture that these studios retooled their brand to promote competitive performance.

7. "The Illini" (or simply "Illini") is a shortform or nickname for the University of Illinois athletic teams and can (and does) refer to any member of the University of Illinois

community—student, fan, alum—and is commonly modified to indicate special-interest groups, like the Dancing Illini, the University's ballroom dance club.

8. This is not to say that competitions are not fun, or that competitive dancers do not have fun, but that the marketing of lessons is rhetorically scaffolded differently, with language that plays up the athleticism, work, and prestige of highly specialized training over the fun factor. Retired competition dancer William pointed out the economic success of David's model when I asked him if he would ever consider teaching ballroom. "If I could do anything, if I was in the stage of having to support myself, the [noncompetition] model that Dave has [provides] a much larger chance of making significant volumes of money than any other model I've seen. And I don't understand why more people haven't adopted it. But once you see it, it's obvious. It's much easier to make money off a hundred people in the class than two."

9. Exhibition and competition ballroom has received more attention in the academic literature. For more on competition and exhibition ballroom, see Ericksen (2011); McMains (2006); Malnig (1992, 2009); Marceau (1998); Marion (2008); Penny (1997, 1999); and Picart (2006).

10. Juliet McMains (2006, 64) makes an important observation when she describes competitive dance as "representations of social dance," as distinct from actual "social dance," and notes that the ballroom dance industry, motivated by increased revenues, rarely recognizes the distinction. I would add that this position is not consistent across ballroom dance contexts. The amateur social dancers I worked with occasionally marked themselves with regard to the categories of competitor and social dancer.

11. In contemporary contexts, successful competition couples who also happen to be married to each other always receive a special recognition of this fact, as if the marriage authenticates the chemistry and legitimates the intimacy performed on the floor. Irene Castle suggested as much when accounting for her success dancing alongside her husband, Vernon Castle: "We were clean-cut; we were married and when we danced there was nothing suggestive about it. We made dancing look like the fun it was. . . . If Vernon had looked into my eyes with smoldering passion during the tango, we both would have burst out laughing" (1980, 86–87). As Castle suggests, removing the sexualized and sensationalized elements of performance typical of other exhibition dancers of the day authenticated their performance as being one between an actual (white, upper-class) husband and wife rather than actors playing roles.

12. Grounded cognitive neuroscience studies are presenting evidence that the act of moving one's body and observing another's movements might be closer than ever imagined. Brain scans of various animal species suggest that the brain activates in similar ways whether a being is actually performing the movement itself or observing another doing so (Gallese et al. 1996; Rizzolatti and Sinigaglia 2008; Zbikowski 2012).

13. See McMains (2006) for more on the emergence of the American style during the mid-1900s.

14. Class is always entangled in regionalism. While it is generally the case that urban contexts are privileged as the more cosmopolitan and elite centers for North American cultural life, as is the case for these dancers, it is also the case that scholarship on the North American performing arts tends to reinforce this bias in documenting and analyzing urban practices (Ned Seelye's culture with a "big C" [1984, 19]) and then projecting their realities on the rest of the country. On the other hand, conventional anthropological work on the performing arts has privileged rural locales often presented as "exotic," presumably more authentic, and far removed from the American mainstream. Ballroom, like many middlebrow practices, resides in an untenable position in this ideological framework, too suburban

and middle class for consideration within scholarship on the performing arts but not low enough (as in not rural or marginalized enough) for consideration as an anthropological subject. This condition has changed over recent decades, aided by the thriving of cultural studies and performance studies scholarship, but an ideological residue still informs the collective intellectual habits on this topic, a fact substantiated by a cursory review of the subjects taught in dance departments across U.S. universities.

15. The World DanceSport Federation has a similar representation, called the Dance Classification Guide, available for download from their official website, which directs the user to this link: http://dance.plussed.net/guides/Dance_Classification_Guide_24.pdf (accessed May 28, 2013). This document also reveals disagreement and some confusion regarding the use of certain terminology, further evidence that even though the public face of the WDSF suggests a strictly codified practice, the discourses surrounding ballroom dance are typified by negotiation and change.

16. Closed position is a dance position in which the leader's right hand is placed on his partner's back while he holds her right hand in his left at eye level. This formation is iconic of ballroom dance and is used in graphic art to depict the genre. Open position is achieved by releasing one or both hands. The WDSF dance classification suggests that the use of closed position is one of the distinguishing characteristics of the Standard dances. Incidentally, the WDSF also uses the term "progressive" to denote traveling dances.

17. Originally the cha cha was called the cha cha chá. While in some formal instances the older name is still in use, the abbreviated cha cha is the more common ballroom referent. It is the form I use throughout this manuscript when talking about its performance in the ballroom, which provides a handy form of distinction from its original Latin American counterpart.

18. The samba was treated as a spot dance at the Regent, while in competitive practice it is considered in some official sources to be a traveling (otherwise known as progressive) dance, even though the basic step does not propel the dancer forward, as is the case for the Standard traveling dances.

19. Ballroom dancers were considered more legitimate for the formal training they undertook, and they were often asked to judge in social competitions at parks, festivals, and so forth, regardless of their lack of expertise in the genre in question. In fact, the use of judges with little knowledge of the genre (perceived to be a sign of neutrality) is not an uncommon aspect of music and dance competitions around the world, and it is a phenomenon worthy of study.

20. This is aligned with Bourdieu's analysis (1984) that suggests that restraint, slowness, and impassivity, which signify elevation in upper-class gesture, are often juxtaposed against the perceived agitation and gesticulation of lower classes. Historically, members of the upper classes have often interpreted a particular brand of participatory ethos in music and dance performance as described by Turino (2008) as a signifier of lower-class sensibilities and status.

21. In his anthropological analysis of Arthur Murray ballroom dance studios, Edward Myers rightly notes that the namesakes of bronze, silver, and gold are applied as metaphors for what is "better," ordering standards and articulating the social significance of dance steps. This commodification of steps endows them with the cultural values of personal advancement, progress, and competition, and it successfully asserts their commercial value in the marketplace (1984, 79–80).

Myers's work is based on his anthropological fieldwork in Arthur Murray dance studios. While both Arthur Murray Inc. and the Regent are commercial venues that teach ballroom dance with significant overlap in terms of their curricular content, their approach (both in terms of teaching and in commerce) is quite different. The Arthur Murray approach, a franchised model with more than eight hundred studios internationally, relies on private instruction with hourly rates and the foregrounding of competitive performance. David Lin's approach downplays the competitive aspect of ballroom performance, highlighting social fun and physical pleasure in the context of large group classes.

22. See also Myers (1979) for a structuralist analysis of the phrase structure of the foxtrot.

23. In fact, students in the Regent classes did not rely on any written notes, notation, or texts at all. It was learned by verbal description, demonstration, and rote repetition.

CHAPTER 2. RULES OF ENGAGEMENT

1. While competition "insiders" attest to the predominance of homosexual males at the higher levels of performance, amateurs and outsiders are less familiar with this aspect of performance (see Gainor 2007; Marion 2008; McMains 2006). When featured in mass media, the genre is performed by heterosexual couples, and images of dancing heterosexual couples serve as icons of the potential for heterosexual pairings and synchrony of men to women, which is why couple dancing is often featured in romantic films and in prescription drug advertisements for sexual dysfunction as the whirling heterosexual couples serve as evidence of the drug's ability to rehabilitate sexual desire and performance.

2. Scholars from a variety of fields and perspectives have addressed this topic; see, for example, Appadurai (1990, 1996); Erlmann (1993); Guilbault (1993); and Monson (1999).

3. In her discussion of competitive ballroom dance, Juliet McMains (2006) highlights the role of "glamour" as a machine through which dancesport is produced. Her discussion of the commodification of glamour through dance and its related industries, along with Myers's (1984) analysis of the commodification of ballroom, provide an important backstory to the construction of beauty in social ballroom dance. McMains's work, along with that of Myers (1984) and Picart (2006), also demonstrate the distance between the competitive and social realms of ballroom performance.

4. In fact, David has often commented that the reason that many dance studios exist in precarious financial circumstances is because most studio owners are dancers first and business owners second. He often talked of franchising, or opening several other branches in nearby towns. Suggesting that if he did he would hire business-savvy managers and teach them how to dance. Teaching dancers how to run a business, David suggested, is a much more difficult proposition. But he was always on the lookout for proficient dancers with a mind for business who would be good candidates to bring into his business as teachers and possible business partners.

5. The point can be taken a step further if we note the pervasive concern for sweat. Dancing causes perspiration, a reality that dress clothes are not ideally suited to address. In fact, the fabrics of dress clothes are either more likely to cause one to perspire or to make it more evident that one is perspiring. During Friday night dances, it was not unusual for men, in particular, to keep several shirts in their car so they could change into a fresh one. Technological advances in athletic wear have helped manufacturers create more breathable fabrics, but social dancers prefer to wear dress clothes that are more constricting and stifling. The class-based signifiers of the dress code, as well as the distance from need articulated by a lack of concern for sweat, takes primacy over physical comfort.

6. There were generally equal numbers of men and women in classes. In the instances where there was more of one than the other, David would space them in such a way that no one danced alone more than once before being paired with another partner. The Friday night dances occasionally saw more a few more women than men in attendance, but this was not generally a rule, and in fact it was often the reverse.

7. Required partner exchange in classes is not a codified aspect of ballroom pedagogy, and although it was required in all the dance studios in the region, it is not consistent across

the country. Competitive ballroom dancers work with only one partner, and studios that promote competitive ballroom dancing are structured around private lessons for established couples. Furthermore, I have talked to a number of social dance instructors from around the country who choose not to require partner exchange. They know their clients are nervous about changing partners, and so they do not require it of them.

8. See Aldrich's (1991) compilation of primary source documents on nineteenth-century social dance for examples of how women were charged with maintaining a safe space by carefully crafting the guest list and the movement of bodies on the floor for private salon dances.

9. Admittedly, my self-selected sample of Regent dancers did not include those who dropped out after a few classes. I did not conduct research with those who expressly quit, and I cannot say if they found the pace of the classes staid. I did not collect statistics on the Regent's retention rates, although anecdotal evidence suggests that they are high.

10. One Regent teacher, Dwight, introduced a new element to the class dynamic that was so successful, David Lin considered codifying it across the curriculum. During one class, instructors usually introduce material for two to three dance genres. After completing the lesson for the first dance of the class, Dwight encouraged his students to give themselves a round of applause as they transitioned into the lesson for the next dance. "It seems like such a small thing," said David, "and a little goofy to me at first, but his students seem to love it. I think moving in that new way and the sound of their own clapping energizes them in a different way." The applause also serves to affirm a sense of accomplishment and mastery of the new movement.

11. In certain moves the woman is in the forward-moving position, and when I performed such moves, I alerted my partner with a slight pressure with the fingers of my left hand when another couple entered our line of dance unexpectedly; my partner generally took note and changed our direction. This was not necessarily standardized, however, and some women did not take on this role when dancing forward.

12. One of my students, Elena Dunckel, has suggested that perhaps the women who preferred to dance with Howard did so because they felt they have performed beauty, that successfully executing a difficult dance and being the object of many onlookers, as is often the case for Howard, allowed these dancers to feel more graceful and more coveted. I am inclined to say she is on to something, and that it connects most specifically with my argument about flow in the concluding chapter herewith, but I did not specifically interview Howard's dance partners on this point.

13. This is not to say that Regent ballroom dancers never drink alcohol or take drugs, but they generally do not do so in excess when dancing.

14. One small group of Regent dancers who socialized together often gathered in the well-appointed suburban home of one of its members to socialize, dance, and drink, In these private contexts, they consumed more alcohol and achieved a state of intoxication that, while not drunk, would have been inappropriate at the Regent. They occasionally complained that they could not meet for drinks prior to attending the Regent classes.

15. David suggested that ballroom dance has the potential to level ethnic and cultural differences, as well as reveal an inherent quality of one's character: "Going out dancing, well, like the early days in disco, it was difficult because there were very few Asians. Sometimes [women] say "No" to you. And I don't know if they don't want to dance with me because I am Chinese or their feet hurt or whatever. But generally, once they dance with me they are pleasantly surprised. "You are on time, you can lead" [he laughs]. That's a good way to start the communication because I really think women can tell by the way they dance with you what kind of person you are. Are you a kind person, or are you a selfish person? Once you

dance they kind of know you, and they either want to continue to talk with you or think, "No, we have nothing in common."

16. *Habitus*, a concept associated with French sociologist and practice theorist Pierre Bourdieu, is useful for understanding identity and the way it is rooted in personal and social habits. It was a response to earlier theories that portrayed culture as relatively fixed over time and neglected to account for cultural change. Bourdieu defined habitus as "systems of durable and transposable dispositions, structured structures predisposed to function as structuring structures" (1972, 72). For a primer on habitus and the work of Bourdieu, see Swartz (1997).

17. See Christopher Small (1996) for a critique of western European art music relative to Eastern and African musical traditions.

CHAPTER 3. COHERENCE TO THE SENSUOUS LIFE

1. For more on gender and social couple dance, see also the work of Ericksen (2011); Hutchinson (2013); Leib and Bulman (2009); Penny (1997); Malnig (1992, 1997, 1999, 2009); Marion (2008); McMains (2006); Savigliano (1995); Skinner (2008); Tomko (1999).

2. On a number occasions David mentioned that while he was not necessarily homophobic, he did imagine that a great many of his clients might be and that they would not be comfortable dancing with a partner of the same sex. Given that his pedagogical model requires participants to rotate partners—it was a non-negotiable component of his approach—he would be requiring all the students to consent to same-sex performance. Doing so, he thought, would result in many of his regular clients quitting and taking his livelihood with him. Whether this would actually transpire is not clear to me. I never talked to him about another possibility, that of creating courses and dance events specifically for same-sex couples. I suspect that were they profitable, he would consider doing so, but do not know for sure. The region also hosted a popular gay bar, C Street, which did offer occasional hustle and salsa nights, although in my experience they usually quickly dissolved into solo dancing.

3. See Gainor (2007) for more on gender in Equality Dance and other same sex ballroom contexts.

4. I would also urge caution for scholars who have interpreted the act of following in dance through their own cultural lenses that attribute a passivity to the act.

5. My focus on the importance of connectedness and acceptance in ballroom provides a counterpoint to the more typical, sexualized language used in the academy and in popular culture with regard to couple dancing. Words like passion, sex, sensuality, desire, and addiction used in scholarly publishing, reviews of performances, and reality television shows reduce couple dancing to an expression of sexual desire and a loss of rational thought. While successful in making the topic of ballroom dance appealing and marketable, such titillating language fails to adequately capture common practice as it occurs on the dance floors for social dancers across the United States. Ballroom dance is not entirely devoid of signs of sexuality, but the Freudian reduction of any kind of physical synchrony and connection to sex is extremely problematic. In my experience with American social ballroom dancers, the kinds of connection they sought through performance were more often something other than sex—or, perhaps better stated, something more than sex. Intimacy, connection, acceptance—even when in physical contexts—are not only about sex. It would behoove scholars to avoid this common pitfall of social discourse, especially for those of us hoping to understand the role of couple dance in American social life. Social cohesion relies on gender and sexuality, but not exclusively. Some types of public dancing and some types of contexts for public dancing are framed differently than courtship contexts (Bateson 1972;

Bauman 1977; Geertz 1973). Participants are well aware of the different types of frames with which to understand different types of couple dance performances, and as scholars we should be more attentive to such distinctions as well.

6. From Amazon plot synopsis, amazon.com, accessed June 12, 2006.

CHAPTER 4. PERFORMING RACE, REMAKING WHITENESS

1. Originally developed by the linguist Roman Jakobson (Jakobson 1978, 1983; Jakobson and Halle 1971; Jakobson and Waugh 1979) and other members of the Prague School, the theory of markedness initially emerged in the field of phonology to account for the literal marking of phonetic symbols in transcriptions to indicate additional phonological features, and over time the theory proved useful in distinguishing between basic and less-common signifiers. Horse, for example, is unmarked because it can refer to both male and female animals, whereas mare is marked because it can refer only to female horses. The concept's utility has been expanded beyond linguistics to many areas of cultural studies in the humanities and social sciences as a means for demonstrating the pervasive power of dominant groups to define the terms of social reality——the common-sense and natural ways of identifying and distinguishing members of a social group, especially with regard to gender and race (see, for example, Phelan 1993). For example, in general parlance, white Americans generally refer to themselves with the unmarked label, American, while the racially marked terms African American or black American are predominantly used to refer to African Americans.

2. The terms Standard and Latin are the competition divisions for international dancesport performance. They were also the terms used most commonly at my fieldsite, even though Regent dancers performed American style. They also used the terms "Modern" and "Smooth" interchangeably with "Standard," but very rarely used the term "Rhythm" for the Latin category. I have chosen to use the language of my informants, understanding that it is in contradiction to the language of dancesport competitors.

3. David suggests as much when asked about how his Chinese identity intersects with dancing: "With my Chinese friends, students, many of whom are professors, or whatever, if I speak Chinese, right away there are special manners, etiquettes and roles I have to play. When I am speaking English we are equal. You know, so they see me, so I only speak English to them. They see me, and they don't know that I can still speak Chinese. So they think, "Well, you've been here too long, and so you're just American." They expect me to act like an American. So, that is perfect. I try to be as American as possible.

4. Of course, competition fashions have and will continue to change. Those presented here are what was typical during the time of my fieldwork.

5. Most ballroom dances begin in closed position, that is, with the man and woman facing each other in a loose embrace. The man holds his partner's right hand in his left hand, and the two are held at her eye level. His left arm wraps around the woman and rests in the space between her waist and her left shoulder blade, on the back of her ribcage. The woman places her left hand on her partner's right shoulder. This position, and the space created between the partners in this position, is called their "frame." Closed position varies slightly from dance to dance, and, of course, from dancer to dancer. The frame is larger in dances such as the waltz and foxtrot, but smaller and "more relaxed" in the rumba and cha cha. In the Latin dances the elbows are lower, more bent, and held in closer to the body. A number of moves, especially in the Latin genres, require the lead to release the hand of his partner. When this happens, the couple is then said to be in open position.

6. Desmond (1997), Oliver (2002), and McMains (2006) use the term "brownface" to denote this type of performance and others like it. While I do not use the term myself, it

is not without merit, and its reference of minstrelsy's blackface is justified, especially with regard to competition ballroom dance.

7. This tendency to equate complex rhythmic counterpoint with racialized physicality and disorder is not uncommon and was rampant throughout the writings of the colonizers of Africa and Latin America.

8. This aesthetic discourse of refinement and control, which posits the overwhelming difficulty of even seemingly simple expressive conventions, is similar to that found in other genres associated with Western European upper-class societies, especially classical music.

9. There are also other reasons for this, based on the way differing ethnicities are valued in contemporary multiculturalist discourse of educated, liberal, elite Americans, where European ancestry can be perceived as a liability (see Gans 1979; Lieberson and Waters 1998; Sacks and Lindholm 2002; Waters 1990).

10. See Bourdieu (1977; 1984) on the importance of redundancy in different spheres of social life.

CHAPTER 5. JOY, FLOW, AND PERSONAL TRANSFORMATION

1. This is not to imply that the genre does not carry the potential for work or drudgery. For instance, ballroom dance professionals, who rely on the performance and teaching of dance for their livelihoods, might not derive any pleasure from the genre at certain points in their careers. Spouses and children who are coerced, if not forced, into ballroom dancing by their mates or parents may also respond with antipathy. My fieldwork did not include any child competitors. The Regent did occasionally offer summer classes to school-age children, and, in fact, I taught such a class in the middle of my fieldwork. The Lins had three school-age children, and such classes were usually offered in connection with the interests and activities of one of their kids but were not otherwise a regular staple at the Regent.

2. In his analysis of salsa dance, Skinner (2008) has suggested that leaders are less likely to enter flow states than followers. My research does not necessarily bear this out, but I am inclined to agree that flow states may be more difficult to achieve for beginner leaders who have yet to habituate the sequences of moves and leadership technique necessary for flow. The learning curve for leaders is frontloaded, and, therefore, finding the optimal balance of challenge—of being able to act with voluntary fiat in the time frame of the music—is generally difficult for beginners. The notion that women just need to keep their hands in the correct position and they will flow through the motion, as indicated by Skinner's informants, does not jibe entirely with my own experiences and the hundreds of conversations I have had with followers on the subject. Although perhaps the case in ideal circumstances, in daily practice with social dancers there are as many, if not more, opportunities for followers to "fall out" of a flow state relative to leaders given the voluntary fiat of a follower may be disrupted by the will of a leader who signals a different move than anticipated.

3. In fact, the Yule Ball in the film *Harry Potter and the Goblet of Fire* (2005) presents viewers with one such alternative. The scene features a Viennese waltz in which the individuals within the heterosexual couples rapidly switch from the follower to leader position in sync with the phrasing of the song (http://www.youtube.com/watch?v=HmZxI8tXVu8).

4. See also Ericksen 2011.

5. In writing about her personal experience recovering from a stroke, brain scientist Jill Bolte Taylor describes in great detail the temporary silencing of the internal analytical voice that accompanied the brain damage to her left hemisphere. Throughout the text she describes the "divine bliss" that she found in the absence of the judgment of her internal critical voice (2006, 110). "Swathed in an enfolding sense of liberation and transformation,

. . . I loved the feeling of deep inner peace that flooded the core of my being" (49, 82). Since her recovery, her research has been directed toward helping individuals cultivate such positive states in healthy ways.

APPENDIX

1. Closed position is a couple dance position in which the right arm of the man encircles his partner's waist and his left hand holds his partner's right. In open position, the man releases his partner's right hand and the two open to face in the same direction (as opposed to facing each other as in closed position).

2. These three percussion instruments, the cuíca (a friction drum), the surdo (a side-slung bass drum), and pandeiro (a frame drum akin with metal rattles similar to the tambourine) are the three identifying instruments of the genre. For more on Brazilian samba, see Behague 1980; Browning 1995; McGowan and Pessanha 1991; Raphael 1990.

3. For more on salsa, see these selected readings: Aparicio 1998; Boggs 1992; Hosokawa 2002; Hutchinson 2013; Román-Velázquez 2002; Washburne 2008; Waxer 1994, 2002a, 2002b. Merengue was a companion genre of sorts; see Austerlitz 1997 for more information.

REFERENCES

Aguilar, John. 1981. "Insider Research: An Ethnography of a Debate." In *Anthropologists at Home in North America: Methods and Issues in the Study of One's Own Society*, edited by Donald A. Messerschmidt, 15–28. Cambridge: Cambridge University Press.

Aldrich, Elizabeth. 1991. *From the Ballroom to Hell: Grace and Folly in Nineteenth-Century Dance*. Evanston, Ind.: Northwestern University Press.

Anderson, Benedict. 1983. *Imagined Communities: Reflections on the Origin and Spread of Nationalism*. London: Verso.

Aparicio, Frances. 1998. *Listening to Salsa: Gender, Latin Popular Music, and Puerto Rican Cultures*. Hanover, N.H.: Wesleyan University Press.

Appadurai, Arjun. 1990. "Disjuncture and Difference in the Global Cultural Economy." *Public Culture* 2, no. 2: 1–24.

———. 1993. "The Heart of Whiteness." *Callaloo* 16, no. 4: 796–807.

———. 1996. *Modernity at Large: Cultural Dimensions of Globalization*. Minneapolis: University of Minnesota Press.

Austerlitz, Paul. 1997. *Merengue: Dominican Music and Dominican Identity*. Philadelphia: Temple University Press.

Averill, Gage. 2003. *Four Parts, No Waiting: A Social History of American Barbershop Quartet*. Oxford: Oxford University Press.

Barz, Gregory, and Timothy Cooley. 2008. *Shadows in the Field: New Perspectives for Fieldwork in Ethnomusicology*. Oxford: University of Oxford Press.

Bateson, Gregory. 1972. *Steps to an Ecology of Mind: A Revolutionary Approach to Man's Understanding of Himself*. New York: Ballantine.

Bauman, Richard. 1971. "Differential Identity and the Social Base of Folklore." *Journal of American Folklore* 84, no. 331: 31–41.

———. 1977. *Verbal Art as Performance*. Rowley, Mass.: Newbury House.

Becker, Judith. 2004. *Deep Listeners: Music, Emotion and Trancing*. Bloomington: University of Indiana Press.

Béhague, Gerard. 1980. "Brazilian Musical Values of the 1960s and 1970s: Popular Urban Music from Bossa Nova to Tropicalia." *Journal of Popular Culture* 14, no. 3: 437–52.

Berger, Harris M. 2009. *Stance: Ideas about Emotion, Style, and Meaning for the Study of Expressive Culture*. Middletown, Conn.: Wesleyan University Press.

Berrios-Miranda, Marisol. 2003. "Bailando salsa en la sala: Como aprendimos a bailar y a vivir" (Dancing Salsa in the Living Room, How we Learned to Dance and to Live). Paper presented at the Annual Meeting for the Society of Ethnomusicology, Miami, Florida.

Blacking, John. 1977. *The Anthropology of the Body*. London: Academic.

———. 1985. "Movement, Dance, Music, and the Venda Girls' Initiation Cycle." In *Society and the Dance: the Social Anthropology of Process and Performance,* edited by Paul Spencer, 64–91. Cambridge: Cambridge University Press.

Boggs, Vernon. 1992. *Salsiology: Afro-Cuban Music and Dance*. New York: Greenwood.

Bosse, Joanna. 1999. "Ballroom Dance: The Problem and Appeal of the Exotic." Paper presented at the Annual Meeting for the Society of Ethnomusicology, Austin, Texas.

———. 2003. "'I Want to Get Ethnic!': White Salsa Dancers and the Pursuit of Ethnicity, Sexuality, and Liberation." Paper presented at the Annual Meeting for the Society of Ethnomusicology, Tempe, Arizona.

———. 2004. "Exotica, Ethnicity, and Embodiment: An Ethnography of Latin Dance in U.S. Popular Culture." PhD diss., University of Illinois at Urbana-Champaign.

———. 2005a. "Performing Whiteness: An Ethnographic Case Study of Ballroom Dance in Central Illinois." Society of Dance History Scholars Proceedings, edited by Susan Cook.

———. 2005b. "To Lead and Follow: Gender, Dominance, and Connection in Ballroom Dance." Paper presented at the Annual Meeting of the Society for Ethnomusicology, Atlanta.

———. 2007a. "Whiteness and the Performance of Race in American Ballroom Dance." *Journal of American Folklore* 120, no. 475: 19–47.

———. 2007b. "Dance in Hollywood Film: Class, Race, and Narratives of Transformation." Paper presented at the Annual Meeting of the Association for Theater in Higher Education, New Orleans.

———. 2008a. "Salsa Dance and the Transformation of Style: An Ethnographic Study of Movement and Meaning in a Cross-Cultural Context." *Dance Research Journal* 40, no 1: 45–64.

———. 2008b. "At the Intersection of Ethnography and Hollywood Film: Ballroom Dance and the Transformation Trope." Paper presented at the Annual Meeting of the Society for Ethnomusicology, Middletown, Conn.

———. 2009. "Small Town Cosmopolitans: Salsa Dance in Rural America." Paper presented at the Annual Meeting of the Society for Ethnomusicology, Midwest Chapter, Minneapolis.

———. 2013a. "Sound Understandings: Embodied Musical Knowledge and 'Connection' in a Ballroom Dance Community." In *Popular Dance and Music Matters,* edited by Sherril Dodds and Susan C. Cook. Burlington, Vt.: Ashgate.

———. 2013b. "Small-Town Cosmopolitans: Salsa Dance in the American Midwest." In *Salsa World: A Global Dance in Local Contexts,* edited by Sydney Hutchinson. Philadelphia: Temple University Press.

———. 2013c. "Salsa Dance as Cosmopolitan Formation: Cooperation, Conflict, and Commerce in the Midwest United States." *Ethnomusicology Forum* 22, no. 2: 210–31.

Bourdieu, Pierre. 1977. *Outline of a Theory of Practice*. Cambridge: Cambridge University Press.

———. 1984. *Distinction: A Social Critique of the Judgment of Taste*. Cambridge, Mass.: Harvard University Press.

Braun, Werner. 1996. "History of International Organized DanceSport." World DanceSport Federation (formerly International DanceSport Federation). Originally published online at http://www.idsf.net.

Browning, Barbara. 1995. *Samba: Resistance in Motion.* Bloomington: Indiana University Press.

Butler, Judith. (1990) 1999. *Gender Trouble: Feminism and the Subversion of Identity.* New York: Routledge.

Caccia, Maria. 2006. "Jerry Springer on Dancing with the Stars: Pre-judge Not." *Blog Critics.* Available at http://blogcritics.org /jerry-springer-on-dancing-with-the (accessed April 19, 2014).

Castle, Irene. 1980. *Castles in the Air.* New York: Da Capo.

Castle, Vernon, and Irene Castle. 1914. *Modern Dancing.* New York: Harper.

Comaroff, Jean, and John Comaroff. 1993. *Modernity and Its Malcontents: Ritual and Power in Postcolonial Africa.* Chicago: University of Chicago Press.

Cook, Susan C. 1998. "Passionless Dancing and Passionate Reform: Respectability, Modernism, and the Social Dancing of Irene and Vernon Castle." In *The Passion of Music and Dance: Body, Gender, and Sexuality,* edited by William Washabaugh, 133–50. Oxford: Berg.

Csikszentmihalyi, Mihaly. 1990. *Flow: The Psychology of Optimal Experience.* New York: Harper and Row.

———. 1988. "The Flow Experience and Its Significance for Human Psychology." In *Optimal Experience: Psychological Studies of Flow in Consciousness,* edited by Mihaly Csikszentmihalyi and Isabella Selega Csikszentmihalyi, 15–35. Cambridge: Cambridge University Press.

Csikszentmihalyi, Mihaly, and Stith Benett. 1971. "An Exploratory Model of Play." *American Anthropologist* 73, no. 1: 45–58.

Csikszentmihalyi, Mihaly, and Isabella Selega Csikszentmihalyi. 1988. *Optimal Experience: Psychological Studies of Flow in Consciousness.* Cambridge: Cambridge University Press.

Daniel, Yvonne. 1995. *Rumba: Dance and Social Change in Contemporary Cuba.* Bloomington: Indiana University Press.

Deloria, Philip. 1998. *Playing Indian.* New Haven, Conn.: Yale University Press.

Desmond, Jane. 1997. *Meaning in Motion: New Cultural Studies of Dance.* Durham, N.C.: Duke University Press.

Dixon-Stowell, Brenda. 1988. "Popular Dance in the Twentieth Century." In *Black Dance from 1619 to Today,* edited by Lynne Fauley Emery, 339–66. Hightstown, N.J.: Princeton Book Co.

Dyer, Richard. 1992. *Only Entertainment.* New York: Routledge.

———. 1997. *White.* London: Routledge.

Ericksen, Julia A. 2011. *Dance with Me: Ballroom Dancing and the Promise of Instant Intimacy.* New York: New York University Press.

Erlmann, Veit. 1992. "'The Past Is Far and the Future Is Far': Power and Performance among Zulu Migrant Workers." *American Ethnologist* 19, no. 4: 688–709.

———. 1993. "The Politics and Aesthetics of Transnational Musics." *World of Music* 35, no. 2: 3–15.

Feld, Steven. 1984. "Sound Structure as Social Structure." *Ethnomusicology* 28, no. 3: 383–409.

———. 1988. "Aesthetics as Iconicity of Style; or, Lift-up-over Sounding: Getting into the Kaluli Groove." *Yearbook for Traditional Music* 20: 74–113.

Foster, Susan Leigh, ed. 1995. *Choreographing History.* Bloomington: University of Indiana Press.

———. 1996. *Corporealities: Dancing, Knowledge, Culture and Power*. London: Routledge.
Frankenburg, Ruth, ed. 1997. *Displacing Whiteness: Essays in Social and Cultural Criticism*. Durham, N.C.: Duke University Press.
Friedson, Stephen. 1996. *Dancing Prophets: Musical Experience in Tumbuka Healing*. Chicago: University of Chicago Press.
Gainor, Ellen. 2007. "'But Who Leads?' Same-Sex Ballroom Dance and the Heteronormative Paradigm." Paper presented at the Annual Meeting of the Association for Theater in Higher Education, New Orleans.
Gallese, Vittorio, Luciano Fadiga, Leonardo Fogassi, and Giacomo Rizzolatt. 1996. "Action Recognition in the Premotor Cortex." *Brain* 119, no. 2: 593–609.
Gans, Herbert J. 1979. Symbolic Ethnicity. *Ethnic and Racial Studies* 2: 1–20.
Geertz, Clifford. 1973. *The Interpretation of Cultures*. New York: Basic.
Giddens, Anthony. 1979. *Central Problems in Social Theory*. Berkeley: University of California Press.
Gorfain, Phyllis. 1993. "When Nothing Really Matters: Body Puns in Hamlet." In *Bodylore*, edited by Katharine Young, 59–87. Knoxville: University of Tennessee Press.
Grossberg, Lawrence. 1992. "Articulation and Culture." In *We Gotta Get Out of This Place: Popular Conservatism and Postmodern Culture*, 37–68. New York: Routledge.
Guilbault, Jocylene. 1993. "On Redefining the 'Local' through World Music." *The World of Music* 35, no. 2: 3–15.
Hagedorn, Katherine. 2001. *Divine Utterances: The Performance of Afro-Cuban Santería*. Washington: Smithsonian Institution Press.
Hahn, Tomie. 2007. *Sensational Knowledge: Embodying Culture through Japanese Dance*. Middletown, Conn.: Wesleyan University Press.
Harris, Trudier. 1995. "Genre." *Journal of American Folklore* 108, no. 430: 509–27.
Henerson, Evan. 2006. "They're Mad about Hot Ballroom Teacher Pierre Dulaine." *Los Angeles Daily News*, April 9. Available at http://www.thefreelibrary.com/THEY%27RE+MAD+ABOUT+HOT+BALLROOM+TEACHER+PIERRE+DULAINE-a0144362030 (accessed July 16, 2009).
Holt, Fabian. 2007. *Genre in Popular Music*. Chicago: University of Chicago Press.
Hood, Mantle. 1960. "The Challenge of Bi-Musicality." *Ethnomusicology* 4, no. 2: 55–59.
Hooper, James. 1991. *Peirce on Signs: Writings on Semiotic by Charles Sanders Peirce*. Chapel Hill: University of North Carolina Press.
Hosokawa, Shuhei. 2002. "Salsa no tiene fronteras: Orquesta de la Luz and the Globalization of Popular Music." In *Situating Salsa: Global Markets and Local Meanings in Latin Popular Music*, edited by Lise Waxer, 289–312. New York: Routledge.
Hutchinson, Syndey, ed. 2013. *Salsa World: A Global Dance in Local Contexts*. Philadelphia: Temple University Press.
Hymes, Dell. 1972. "Toward Ethnographies of Communication: The Analysis of Communicative Events." In *Language and Social Context*, edited by Pier Paolo Giglioli, 21–47. Harmondsworth, Middlesex: Penguin.
Jakobson, Roman. 1978. *Six Lectures on Sound and Meaning*. Cambridge, Mass.: MIT Press.
———. 1983. *Dialogues*. Cambridge, Mass.: MIT Press.
Jakobson, Roman, and Morris Halle. 1971. *Fundamentals of Language*. The Hague: Mouton.
Jakobson, Roman, and Linda Waugh. 1979. *The Sound and Shape of Language*. Bloomington: Indiana University Press.
Kapchan, Deborah A. 1993. "Moroccan Women's Body Signs." In *Bodylore*, edited by Katherine Young, 3–34. Knoxville: University of Tennessee Press.

Keil, Charles. 1987. "Participatory Discrepancies and the Power of Music." *Cultural Anthropology* 2, no. 3: 275–83.

———. 1992. *Polka Happiness.* Philadelphia: Temple University Press.

———. 1995. "The Theory of Participatory Discrepancies: A Progress Report." *Ethnomusicology* 39, no. 1: 1–20.

Keil, Charles, and Steven Feld. 1994. *Music Grooves: Essays and Dialogues.* Chicago: University of Chicago Press.

Kisliuk, Michelle. 1998. *Seize the Dance! BaAka Musical Life and the Ethnography of Performance.* Oxford: Oxford University Press.

Lausevic, Mirjana. 1998. "A Different Village: International Folk Dance and Balkan Music and Dance in the United States." PhD diss., Wesleyan University.

———. 2007. *Balkan Fascination: Creating an Alternative Music Culture in America.* New York: Oxford University Press.

Lea, James. 2001. "Charles Sanders Peirce, the Extraordinary Moment, and Musical Affect." DMA, School of Music, University of Illinois at Urbana-Champaign.

Leib, Allison, and Robert Bulman. 2009. "The Choreography of Gender: Masculinity, Femininity, and the Complex of Identity in Ballroom." *Men and Masculinities* 11, no. 5: 602–21.

Levine-Rasky, Cynthia, ed. 2002. *Working through Whiteness: International Perspectives.* Albany: State University of New York Press.

Lieberson, Stanley, and Mary Waters. 1988. *From Many Strands: Ethnic and Racial Groups in Contemporary America.* New York: Russell Sage Foundation.

Malnig, Julie. 1992. *Dancing till Dawn: A Century of Exhibition Ballroom Dance.* Westport, Conn.: Greenwood.

———. 1997. "Two-Stepping to Glory: Social Dance and the Rhetoric of Social Mobility." *Etnofoor* 10, no. 1/2: 128–50.

———. 1999. "Athena Meets Venus: Visions of Women in Social Dance in the Teens and Early 1920s." *Dance Research Journal* 31, no. 2: 34–62.

———, ed. 2009. *Ballroom, Boogie, Shimmy Sham, Shake: A Social and Popular Dance Reader.* Urbana: University of Illinois Press.

Marceau, Yvonne. 1998. "Ballroom Dance Competition." *International Encyclopedia of Dance.* Oxford: Oxford University Press.

Marcus, George. 1983. *Elites: Ethnographic Issues.* Albuquerque: University of New Mexico.

Marion, Jonathan. 2008. *Ballroom: Culture and Costume in Competitive Dance.* New York: Berg.

McGowan, Chris, and Ricardo Pessanha. 1991. "Samba: The Heartbeat of Rio." Chapter 2 in *The Brazilian Sound: Samba, Bossa Nova and the Popular Music of Brazil.* Philadelphia: Temple University Press.

McMains, Juliet. 2006. *Glamour Addiction: Inside the American Ballroom Dance Industry.* Middletown, Conn.: Wesleyan University Press.

Messerschmidt, Donald A., ed. 1981. *Anthropologists at Home in North America.* Cambridge: Cambridge University Press.

Miller, Carolyn R. 1984. Genre as Social Action. *Quarterly Journal of Speech* 70, no. 2: 151–67.

Moffatt, Michael. 1992. "Ethnographic Writing about American Culture." *Annual Review of Anthropology* 21: 205–29.

Monson, Ingrid. 1999. "Riffs, Repetition, and Theories of Globalization." *Ethnomusicology* 43, no. 1: 31–65.

Moore, Robin. 1995. "The Commercial Rumba: Afrocuban Arts as International Popular Culture." *Latin American Music Review* 16, no. 2: 165–98.

———. 1997. *Nationalizing Blackness: Afrocubanismo and Artistic Revolution in Havana, 1920–1940*. Pittsburgh: University of Pittsburgh Press.

Morin, Richard. 2008. "America's Four Middle Classes." Pew Research Center Publications. Washington: Pew Research Center.

Morris, Rosalind. 1995. "All Made Up: Performance Theory and the New Anthropology of Sex and Gender." *Annual Review of Anthropology* 24, no. 1: 567–92.

Morrison, Toni. 1992. *Playing in the Dark: Whiteness and the Literary Imagination*. Cambridge: Harvard University Press.

Murray, Arthur. 1954. *How to Become a Good Dancer*. New York: Simon and Schuster.

Myers, Edward. 1979. "A Phase-Structural Analysis of the Foxtrot, with Transformational Rules." *Journal for the Anthropological Study of Human Movement* 1, no. 4, 246–68.

———. 1984."Ballroom Dance as a Commodity: An Anthropological Viewpoint." *Journal for the Anthropological Study of Human Movements* 3, no. 2: 74–83.

Negus, Keith. 1996. *Popular Music in Theory*. Middletown, Conn.: Wesleyan University Press.

———. 1999. *Music Genres and Corporate Cultures*. New York: Routledge.

Oliver, Cynthia. 2002. "Winin' yo' wais': The Changing Tastes of Dance on the U.S. Virgin Island of St. Croix. In *Caribbean Dance from Abakua to Zouk: How Movement Shapes Identity*, edited by Susanna Sloat, 199–218. Gainesville: University Press of Florida.

Peirce, Charles Sanders. 1955. *Philosophical Writings of Peirce*. Edited by Justus Buchler. New York: Dover.

———. 1958. *Charles S. Peirce: Selected Writings*. Edited by Philip P. Wiener. New York: Dover.

———. 1960. *The Collected Papers of Charles Sanders Peirce*. Edited by Charles Harshorne and Paul Weiss. Cambridge, Mass.: Belknap.

———. 1991. *Peirce on Signs*. Edited by James Hoopes. Chapel Hill: University of North Carolina Press.

———. 1992. *The Essential Peirce: Selected Philosophical Writings*. Vol. 1. Edited by Nathan Houser and Christian Kloesel. Bloomington: University of Indiana Press.

Peña, Manuel. 1985. "From Ranchero to Jaitón: Ethnicity and Class in Texas-Mexican Music." *Ethnomusicology* 29:29–55.

Penny, Patricia A. 1997. "Contemporary Competitive Ballroom Dancing: An Ethnography." PhD diss., University of Surrey, Surrey, England.

———. 1999. "Dancing at the Interface of the Social and the Theatrical: Focus on the Participatory Patterns of Contemporary Competition Ballroom Dancers in Britain." *Dance Research* (Journal of the Society for Dance Research) 17, no. 1: 47–74.

Phelan, Peggy. 1993. *Unmarked: The Politics of Performance*. New York: Routledge.

Picart, Caroline. 2006. *From Ballroom to DanceSport: Aesthetics, Athletics, and Body Culture*. Albany: State University of New York Press.

Raphael, Alison. 1990. "From Popular Culture to Microenterprise: The History of Brazilian Samba Schools." *Latin American Music Review* 11, no. 1: 73–84.

Rizzolatti, Giacomo, and Corrado Sinigaglia. 2008. *Mirrors in the Brain: How Our Minds Share Actions and Emotions*. Oxford: Oxford University Press.

Roberts, John Storm. (1978) 1999. *The Latin Tinge*. 2nd ed. New York: Original Music.

Roediger, David. 1990. *The Wages of Whiteness: Race and the Making of the American Working Class*. New York: Verso.

Román-Velázquez, Patria. 2002. "Locating Salsa." In *Popular Music Studies*, edited by Keith Negus and David Hesmondhalgh, 210–22. London: Oxford University Press.

Rouget, Gilbert. 1985. *Music and Trance: A Theory of the Relations between Music and Possession.* Chicago: University of Chicago Press.

Sacks, Michael, and Marika Lindholm. 2002. "A Room without a View: Social Distance and the Structuring of Privileged Identity." In *Working through Whiteness: International Perspectives,* edited by Cynthia Levine-Rasky, 129–52. Albany: State University of New York Press.

Said, Edward. (1978) 2003. *Orientalism.* New York: Pantheon.

Savigliano, Marta. 1995. *Tango and the Political Economy of Passion.* Boulder, Colo.: Westview.

Seelye, H. Ned. 1984. *Teaching Culture: Strategies for Intercultural Communication.* Lincolnwood, Ill.: National Textbook.

Skinner, Jonathan. 2008. "Women Dancing Back—and Forth: Resistance and Self-Regulation in Belfast Salsa." *Dance Research Journal* 40, no.1: 65–77.

Sklar, Diedre. 1991. "On Dance Ethnography." *Dance Research Journal* 23, no. 1: 6–10.

———. 2000. "Reprise: On Dance Ethnography." *Dance Research Journal* 32, no. 1: 70–77.

Slobin, Mark. 1993. *Subcultural Sounds: Micromusics of the West.* Hanover, N.H.: University Press of New England.

———. 2000. *Fiddler on the Move: Exploring the Klezmer World.* Oxford: Oxford University Press.

Small, Christopher. (1980) 1996. *Music, Society, Education.* Middletown, Conn.: Wesleyan University Press.

Spiller, Henry. 2010. *Erotic Triangles: Sundanese Dance and Masculinity in West Java.* Chicago: University of Chicago Press.

Stearns, Marshall, and Jean Stearns. 1968. *Jazz Dance: The Story of American Vernacular Dance.* New York: Macmillan.

Strathern, Marilyn. 1987. "The Limits of Auto-Anthropology." In *Anthropology at Home,* edited by Anthony Jackson, 16–37. London: Tavistock.

Sugarman, Jane. 1989. "The Nightingale and the Partridge: Singing and Gender among Prespa Albanians." *Ethnomusicology* 33, no. 2: 191–209.

Swartz, David. 1997. *Culture and Power: The Sociology of Pierre Bourdieu.* Chicago: University of Chicago Press.

Taylor, Jill Bolte. 2006. *My Stroke of Insight: A Brain Scientist's Personal Journey.* New York: Plume.

Taylor, Julie. 1976. "Tango: Theme of Class and Nation." *Ethnomusicology* 20, no. 2: 273–91.

Tomko, Linda. 1999. *Dancing Class: Gender, Ethnicity, and Social Divides in American Dance, 1890–1920.* Bloomington: Indiana University Press.

Trouillot, Michel-Rolph. 1995. *Silencing the Past: Power and the Production of History.* Boston: Beacon.

Turino, Thomas. 1993. *Moving Away from Silence: Music of the Peruvian Altiplano and the Experience of Urban Migration.* Chicago Studies in Ethnomusicology. Series edited by P. Bohlman and B. Nettl. Chicago: University of Chicago Press.

———. 1999. "Signs of Imagination, Identity, and Experience: A Peircian Semiotic Theory for Music." *Ethnomusicology* 43, no. 2: 221–55.

———. 2000. *Nationalists, Cosmopolitans, and Popular Music in Zimbabwe.* Chicago: University of Chicago Press.

———. 2008. *Music as Social Life: The Politics of Participation.* Chicago: University of Chicago Press.

Turino, Thomas, and James Lea. 2004. *Identity and the Arts in Diaspora Communities.* Warren, Mich.: Harmonie Park.

Turner, Victor, and Edward Bruner. 1986. *The Anthropology of Experience*. Urbana: University of Illinois Press.

U.S. Bureau of the Census. 2000. *Census Data for Illinois*. Available at illinoisgis.ito.state.il.us/census2000 (accessed April 22, 2014).

Uba, George Russell. 2007. "From Signifying to Performance: International Ballroom Dance and the Choreographies of Transnationalism." *Journal of Asian American Studies* 10, no. 2: 141–67.

Veloz, Frank, and Yolanda Veloz. 1938. *Tango and Rumba: The Dances of Today and Tomorrow*. New York: Harper.

Wagner, Ann. 1997. *Adversaries of Dance: From the Puritans to the Present*. Urbana: University of Illinois Press.

Washburne, Christopher. 2008. *Sounding Salsa: Performing Latin Music in New York City*. Philadelphia: Temple University Press.

Waters, Mary. 1990. *Ethnic Options: Choosing Identities in America*. Berkeley: University of California Press.

Waxer, Lise. 1994. "Of Mambo Kings and Songs of Love: Dance Music in Havana and New York from the 1930s-1950s." *Latin American Music Review* 15, no. 2: 139–76.

———. 2002a. *The City of Musical Memory: Salsa, Record Grooves, and Popular Culture in Cali, Colombia*. Middletown, Conn.: Wesleyan University Press.

———, ed. 2002b. *Situating Salsa: Global Markets and Locating Meanings in Latin Popular Music*. New York: Routledge.

Wellman, David. 1993. *Portraits of White Racism*. 2nd ed. New York: Cambridge University Press.

———. 1997. "Minstrel Shows, Affirmative Action Talk, and Angry White Men: Marking Racial Otherness in the 1990s." In *Displacing Whiteness: Essays in Social and Cultural Criticism*, edited by Ruth Frankenburg, 311–31. Durham, N.C.: Duke University Press.

West, Cornel. 1993. *Race Matters*. Boston: Beacon.

Zbikowski, Lawrence. 2012. "Music and Movement: A View from Cognitive Science." Draft submission for the symposium volume *Bewegungen zwischen Hören und Sehen* (Movements between Hearing and Seeing), Research Institute for Music Theater, University of Bayreuth.

INDEX

Note: page numbers in *italics* refer to figures and tables.

JOANNA BOSSE is an associate professor of ethnomusicology and dance studies at Residential College in the Arts and Humanities at Michigan State University.